Knitting with
Hand-Dyed Yarns

KNITTING

Missy Burns, Stephanie Blaydes Kaisler, and Anita Tosten

WITH HAND-DYED YARNS

20 Stunning Projects

Martingale® & COMPANY

Knitting with Hand-Dyed Yarns:
20 Stunning Projects
© 2004 by Missy Burns, Stephanie Blaydes Kaisler,
and Anita Tosten

Martingale & Company®
20205 144th Avenue NE
Woodinville, WA 98072-8478
www.martingale-pub.com

Credits

President: Nancy J. Martin

CEO: Daniel J. Martin

Publisher: Jane Hamada

Editorial Director: Mary V. Green

Managing Editor: Tina Cook

Technical Editor: Karen Costello Soltys

Copy Editor: Liz McGehee

Design Director: Stan Green

Illustrator: Robin Strobel

Cover and Text Designer: Stan Green

Model Photographer: John Hamel

Photography Assistant: T. J. Gettings

Hair and Makeup Stylist: Caroline Picking

Studio Photographer: Brent Kane

Mission Statement

Dedicated to providing quality products and service
to inspire creativity.

Printed in China
09 08 07 06 05 04   8 7 6 5 4 3 2 1

Library of Congress Cataloging-in-Publication Data

Burns, Missy.
    Knitting with hand-dyed yarns : 20 stunning projects / Missy Burns, Stephanie Blaydes Kaisler, and Anita Tosten.
        p. cm.
    ISBN 1-56477-553-4
1. Knitting—Patterns. 2. Dyes and dyeing—Textile fibers. I. Kaisler, Stephanie Blaydes. II. Tosten, Anita. III. Title.
    TT825.B875 2004
    746.43'2041—dc22

                                2004012866

Dedication

For our husbands

Acknowledgments

Anita and Missy would like to give special thanks to J. D. Pyshnik, Cheri Roth, and
Rose Wilson—the employees of Wool in the Woods. All three of them picked up the slack
and kept us on schedule while we worked on this book. In addition, each one,
in his or her own way, gave us creative inspiration.

Anita and Missy would also like to thank Dottie Burbol, Dawn Eaton, Cheri Roth,
Rose Stockslager, and Rose Wilson for all of the knitting and finishing they did for this book.
This project would not have been completed without their assistance.

Stephanie would like to thank the staff of The Yarn Garden in Annapolis, Maryland,
for teaching her how to knit.

We would like to thank Baabajoes Wool Company; Blue Heron Yarns; Blue Sky Alpacas, Inc.;
Cherry Tree Hill Yarn; Dancing Fibers; Fiesta Yarns; Great Adirondack Yarn Company; Lorna's Laces;
Mountain Colors; Prism Arts, Inc.; and Schaefer Yarn for their contributions
of yarn and their participation in this project.

Words cannot express our undying gratitude for all of the guidance, creativity, and support
Carol and Ron Woolcock have given us through this project. In fact, we think that it is fair to say
that without their help over the years we would not be in business and, most assuredly,
we would not have had the opportunity to write this book.
We are most fortunate to have such gracious and thoughtful mentors.

We would like to send a special thank you to John Hamel, who did the model photography for
this book. We all feel so fortunate that he shared his talent, good humor, and sense of adventure with
us. In every picture he shot, John captured the beauty of the color and texture of hand-dyed yarn.

Thank you to our guardian angel at Martingale & Company, Karen Soltys. Karen's attention to
detail, superb writing skills, and calm demeanor were helpful beyond measure as we wrote this book.

Last but not least, we would all like to thank Rod Tosten, Anita's husband.
It is through Rod that the authors became friends and colleagues.

Contents

Our Personal Journey to Hand-Dyed Yarn

FEW THINGS ARE MORE BEAUTIFUL, peaceful, and comforting than a walk in the woods. After a short time, all of the senses are heightened and awareness peaks. Suddenly natural beauty comes into focus—the timelessness of nature, the seemingly endless palette of colors, the myriad textures, and how they all combine to make an exquisite and unique place.

FROM A RUSTIC, NATURAL SETTING, Wool in the Woods produces hand-dyed yarns, patterns, and kits. Wool in the Woods studio is nestled in the middle of a woodland setting in south-central Pennsylvania. Set atop a hillside, our studio gives us a peaceful and intoxicating view of the world below.

When you enter Wool in the Woods, you find that the beauty, peace, and comfort of the surrounding woods are repeated inside the studio. The walls and ceiling are made of pine, hickory, and hemlock planks. The studio is an open space with a loft that runs around the outer edges. Skeins of yarn dyed the previous day hang from the loft's banisters. The sunlight streaming into the studio mixes with the colors of the yarn to create a dazzling spectacle of colors that is warm, soft, and inviting.

The most delightful aspect of a visit to Wool in the Woods is meeting the staff. The Wool in the Woods welcoming committee greets all visitors at the door. The committee is made up of Taffy, Tilly, Abby, and Kelby—the pets of the staff. Yes, everyone who works at Wool in the Woods brings his or her pet to work. Wool in the Woods is a busy place. The day begins with the staff wrapping and tagging the hand-dyed yarn to fill customer orders so that the parcels can be shipped that day. Once the orders are filled, the dyeing process begins. While all of this is happening, Missy is managing the external affairs of the company. Though each member of the staff has a specialty, each can pitch in and help complete the day's work in any other part of the company. Everyone is talking and laughing—or barking, in the case of the welcoming committee. In fact, the noise level is a low roar of giggles and laughter. It is obvious to anyone who visits that this is a fun and productive place to work.

Anita Tosten and Missy Burns, owners of Wool in the Woods, set this fun and productive tone. Anita is the creative influence behind the business. Missy is the organizational and business force who keeps the studio together. Though they are remarkably different women in skills and demeanor, Anita's and Missy's personalities are perfect complements. Both women admire the skills and abilities they see in each other. This relationship has grown over the years, because when they first met, Anita and Missy were not fond of each other.

Not fond of each other is a bit of an understatement. Anita and Missy met because their husbands, Rod and Randy, respectively, are best friends from childhood. Anita and Rod had been dating

for a long time when Missy came into Randy's life. Unfortunately, Anita took an immediate dislike to Missy. In fact, she felt so uncomfortable about Missy that she hosted a party for Randy to meet all of her friends who were single women, hoping that Randy would find a more "suitable" mate at the party. Though flattered by Anita's concern and effort, Randy remained smitten with Missy.

Being the good wives that they are, Anita and Missy accompanied their husbands to countless social gatherings and, as a consequence, spent a great deal of time together. Though the friendship did not form initially, a respect for the other person's gifts did. So, in the spring of 1998 when Anita decided she wanted to start a business called "Wool in the Woods," she knew that she would need someone to handle the administrative side of establishing and running a business. Anita asked Missy to be that person. With the formation of the partnership and the creation of Wool in the Woods, a generous and loving friendship grew as well.

So, what brought Anita and Missy to knitting in the first place? It all started because Anita was looking for a new challenge. Nin, her husband's grandmother, suggested that she needed to work with her hands as a creative outlet. Nin always found joy and a sense of peace in her crocheting, so Anita thought she would try crocheting, too. As she entered the Yarn Basket to purchase her first supply of crocheting items, she encountered a large sign that read, "Knitting Classes Starting in September." So, she decided to give knitting a try. With help and encouragement from Nin, Anita found her

creative outlet. She took more knitting classes at the Yarn Basket. In fact, Anita took so many classes and learned the material so thoroughly that the Yarn Basket asked her to teach as well. Because Missy had always admired the garments that Anita knit and wore, she began knitting a few years later.

Anita's creativity blossomed. She began designing clothing that could be worn anywhere—garments that were comfortable, attractive, and made to last a lifetime. Wanting to learn more, she sought further instruction from Carol Woolcock, owner of The Manning's in East Berlin, Pennsylvania. It was Carol who first suggested that Anita learn how to dye yarn. In fact, not only did Carol sell Anita her first book on hand dyeing yarn, she also gave her a crash course in dyeing while Anita was paying for the book.

Anita began dyeing yarn in the basement of her home. She had found her true calling—she just *loved* dyeing yarn—and decided to start up a business. Realizing that she couldn't run a business alone, she asked Missy to be her partner, and Wool in the Woods was born. While Anita and Missy were busy dyeing yarn in Anita's basement and also at Missy's home, Anita's husband, Rod, built the barn that now houses the dyeing studio. Wool in the Woods moved to its current location in 2000.

The mission of Wool in the Woods is to provide unique, quality yarns at a reasonable price. Along with the hand-dyed yarn, Wool in the Woods offers patterns for garments as well as home and fashion accessories. In keeping with Anita's first design, the garments created by Wool in the Woods

can be worn everywhere and will last a long time. Missy is thrilled that Wool in the Woods provides hand-dyed yarn that fellow knitters enjoy using. Anita's delight in the business is a bit different. She says, "I just want to touch yarn all day." Together, Anita and Missy fulfill their dreams and provide knitters everywhere with a temptation to try hand-dyed yarn.

Anita and Missy continue to add people to the Wool in the Woods family. They asked Stephanie to join them to write this book. Stephanie has enjoyed the process because it combines her love of both writing and knitting.

Now the journey begins—your journey to learn how to create a work of art with hand-dyed yarn.

We at Wool in the Woods hope that this book will help you find your own unique creative spirit. For all of us, the studio is a center for our creativity. In fact, when we discuss what we do, we give everyone at Wool in the Woods credit. When we say that we created something, it is always the "BIG We." So "We" hope that as you read and use this book, you will be transported from your living room or den to a place that helps you find your own center of creativity. Perhaps it will feel like driving down a country road and being enveloped by the beauty of a tree-canopied road, a beautiful lake, and the colors and texture of the woods. Soon you will arrive at your creative place that is just like Wool in the Woods. The welcoming committee is waiting.

Left to Right: Stephanie, Anita, and Missy.

Your Journey Begins Here

CONGRATULATIONS! If you're reading these pages, you're tempted to try knitting with hand-dyed yarn, and as a result, you've begun the process to find your own center of creativity with knitting.

WE HOPE THAT THIS BOOK will serve as your point of departure as you embark on your journey into the evolving world of hand-dyed yarn. To all of us, this book will be a success if you use the information and patterns as stepping-stones in your creative journey.

Unlike many other knitting publications, this book is not a "technique" book. By that, we mean that our intent is not to introduce you to new knitting stitches. If you would like to learn a new stitch, please refer to a "how-to" instruction book or a stitch dictionary. What this book offers is a new perspective on some tried-and-true stitches and techniques. When you add the element of hand-dyed yarn to the mix, you gain greater creative opportunities because the texture and color of the hand-dyed yarn transform the stitches you are familiar with into something sensational.

So, why knit with hand-dyed yarn? For us, the answer is simple: you will have endless opportunities to create one-of-a-kind garments. Also, there is the element of surprise. The surprise can be how beautifully colors and textures combine, or how a particular stitch brings out a hue of color by catching the light in a way that you did not expect. Whether you use a multicolored yarn (one dyed with several different colors spaced alternately along the length of the skein) or a monocolored yarn (one that is dyed with one color, yet offers a more mottled effect than a commercial "solid" yarn), the results will be interesting and unique.

Why does hand-dyed yarn provide knitters with the opportunity to knit a unique garment each time they knit? What is the secret that allows a combination of a couple of hand-dyed yarns or the simplest of stitches to become a surprisingly captivating garment? We're often asked these questions. In fact, one of the great mysteries of knitting with hand-dyed yarn is that each knitted item is unique. For instance, two people can use the same pattern, the same hand-dyed yarn, and the same size needles, yet the two sweaters look different. We know that knitting is mathematically based since you count stitches, needles are a certain diameter, and the gauge is based on the number of stitches knit within a specific measurement, so we turned to Dr. James Fink, a professor of mathematics at Gettysburg College, to help us solve the mystery.

The easiest way to answer the question is to break down the art of knitting with hand-dyed yarn into its individual parts: stitch count, length of color, needle size, type of stitch, and the individual knitter. When combined, these individual parts create a knitted garment. As you know, these individual components of knitting can change in any given knitting situation. Because they change or vary, we will call the individual parts "variables."

The first variable, stitch count, is for patterns that require different stitches in the same row. The count is how many times you knit a specific stitch. Length of color is the second variable. When you look at multicolored hand-dyed yarn, you'll notice that the length of each color on the piece of yarn varies. Dye processes differ, and as a consequence there is no standard length.

The third variable is needle size. The size of the stitches directly correlates to the size of the needle. The fourth variable is the type of stitch you are knitting. And, finally, the last variable is the variation that comes with each knitter's personal style of knitting. You cannot knit a garment without these five essential variables. The surprise of knitting with hand-dyed yarn appears when the variables combine to create a knitted garment.

Dr. Fink took each of the five components into consideration during our discussion. He described the knitted garment made of hand-dyed yarn as a function of the five variables discussed above. His answer to our questions is unbelievably simple: because each of the variables is different, when combined, they will always create something unique.

So, the mystery is solved. Each skein of hand-dyed yarn is unique and when combined with each knitter's own style, you will always end up with a one-of-a-kind garment.

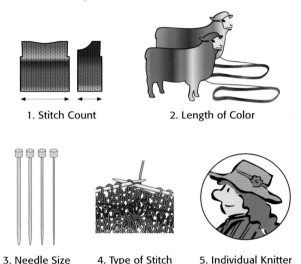

1. Stitch Count   2. Length of Color

3. Needle Size   4. Type of Stitch   5. Individual Knitter

To describe his thoughts a different way, for just a moment, think of the process of knitting as a "mystery machine." In order for the mystery machine to work, it needs to be fed the input materials, the variables discussed above. Once the materials have been input, the mystery machine can work its magic. In combining these variable parts, the mystery machine creates your output, your product. In our case, that product is how the color falls on a knitted garment. The diagram below explains why every garment knit with hand-dyed yarn is unique. Essentially, when you are using hand-dyed yarn, you will always create something unique.

When you are wandering around in a yarn store, looking for hand-dyed yarns, you know that the selection is not only from a wide array of colors and textures, but also from a variety of products made by different companies. So, to make the most exquisite and unique garment, you look for complementary colors and textures. As a consequence, your selections may be a combination of hand-dyed yarns from different companies. The only way we could attempt to duplicate the selection of hand-dyed yarns available at a yarn store was with the help of many of our colleagues in the industry. We would like to thank Baabajoes Wool Company, Blue Heron Yarns, Blue Sky Alpacas, Inc., Cherry Tree Hill Yarn, Dancing Fibers, Fiesta Yarns, Great Adirondack Yarn Company, Lorna's Laces, Mountain Colors, Prism Arts, Inc., and Schaefer Yarn for their generosity in allowing us to use their hand-dyed yarns in this book.

To help with your yarn selections, we've included icons with each project that indicate suitable yarn weight. If you can't find the yarn used in a project, or if you'd like to substitute a yarn, these icons will help you decide which types of yarns would be appropriate. The icons are shown below. For more explanation, turn to the Standard Yarn-Weight System chart on page 110. These weight categories were devised by the Craft Yarn Council of America.

We've also rated each project's skill level to make it easy for you to select which projects you'd like to make. Again, we've based our ratings on the guidelines developed by the Craft Yarn Council. For a full explanation of each skill level, see page 110.

Thank you for reading our book. We hope that it will help you find your center of creativity and that you will develop a love of knitting. Now, let's try that first stepping-stone.

Tips for Working with Hand-Dyed Yarns

IF YOU HAVE KNIT BEFORE, you know that knitting appeals to most of our senses. Hand-dyed yarn is pleasing to the eye. The click-click sound of knitting needles creates a soothing rhythm. Hand-dyed yarn feels wonderful. And, surprisingly enough, some hand-dyed yarns have a distinct scent.

Let It Breathe

Every hand-dyed yarn company has its own secret recipes for dyeing yarn, so different ingredients are used to create the hand-dyed yarns. Some hand-dyed yarns smell like vinegar. Others smell like chemicals. And, some have no odor at all. The best way to get rid of any odor is to let the yarn air out for a while. Often, just the process of knitting your garment will give the hand-dyed yarn plenty of time to air out, and the odor will disappear.

Bleeding

The way that color is set in the yarn differs from company to company, too, since the methods used depend on the types of dyes used. As a result, while you are knitting with some hand-dyed yarn, you may find that the color comes off on your hands. If you knit with wooden or bamboo knitting needles, you will notice that the dye seeps into the wood as well. Never fear—nothing is wrong with the hand-dyed yarn or with how you are handling it. The oils from your skin combined with the heat from your hands and the friction of knitting causes the color to come off onto your hands and knitting needles. The color easily washes off of your hands. But, due to the porous nature of wood and bamboo, your knitting needles will remain the color of the dye.

Like any other item that has been dyed—leather for purses, shoes, and garments or fabric for turtlenecks and sweatshirts—sometimes the dye will come through while you are wearing the garment. Although this is unusual, it does happen. You can prevent it by prewashing the garment, using the instructions on the yarn's label.

Blending Colors

One virtue of hand-dyed yarn is that the colors are not intended to be uniform throughout a skein or dye lot of yarn. Color variation is what makes hand-dyed yarn so spectacular.

If you are knitting a garment that requires more than one skein of the same hand-dyed yarn, you will want to ensure that the colors from all of the skeins are blended throughout the garment. The easiest and most effective way to accomplish this thorough level of blending is to alternate skeins as you knit the garment. For example, let's say that you are knitting a garment that requires six skeins of the same hand-dyed yarn. Instead of knitting straight through one skein and then starting with the next, why not knit a couple of inches or rows from each skein in sequence so that the variations in color are further blended throughout the sweater. Essentially, if you do not alternate skeins, you will not see all of the colors of all of the skeins throughout the garment.

One of the easiest ways to work with multiple skeins is to label each skein numerically or alphabetically. So, first you would knit a certain length,

which is sometimes suggested in the pattern, using skein 1. Then you would knit an equal amount using skein 2 and so on until the garment is complete. When we label our skeins, whether they are wound by hand or with a ball winder, we use two different methods: we put a rubber band around the ball of yarn and stick a label in between the rubber band and the hand-dyed yarn, or we put each skein in its own plastic zippered bag with a label. When your project is complete, all of the color variations will have been blended to make your one-of-a-kind garment.

Basic Finishing Techniques

WHEN IT COMES TO FINISHING your hand-dyed garments, you'll want the finishing techniques you use to look just as professional as the rest of your knitting. Below, you'll find step-by-step instructions for our favorite techniques.

Long-Tail Cast On

Make a slipknot on one needle, leaving a yarn tail equal to roughly 1" for every stitch you need to cast on.

1. Wrap the long yarn tail around your left thumb and the yarn that's connected to the ball or skein around your index finger. Then hold both yarn ends in the palm of your hand with your remaining fingers.

2. Slip the tip of the needle under the loop on the thumb, then (without slipping this loop off of the needle), bring the tip over the top of the loop on your index finger.

3. Use the needle to pull the index-finger loop through the thumb loop. Let go of both yarn ends and tighten the resulting loop gently on the needle. (Do not pull too tightly or you will have a cast-on edge that is tight and inflexible.) You've just cast on one stitch.

4. Repeat steps 1–3 until you have cast on the desired number of stitches, noting that the original slipknot counts as one stitch.

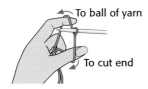

Three-Needle Bind Off

Rather than binding off each shoulder edge and then sewing the front and back shoulders together, we often like to knit the shoulders together. This technique requires that you keep the remaining shoulder stitches on a holder rather than binding them off. Then, when you're ready to join the front to the back, you bind off the front and back together to create a join that is less bulky than a sewn seam.

1. Hold the front and back of the knitted fabric right sides together with the needles parallel.

2. Insert a third needle into the first stitch on each of the left-hand needles. Knit these stitches together.

Right sides together, knit together one stitch from front needle and one stitch from back needle.

3. Insert the right-hand needle into the next stitch on both left-hand needles. Knit these stitches together. There are now two stitches on the right-hand needle. Bind off one stitch.

Bind off.

4. Repeat steps 2 and 3 until all stitches are bound off.

Buttonholes

1. Place a marker at the desired location of each buttonhole.

2. Work as established to marker. Bind off the required number of stitches for the size of the button. (The pattern instructions will generally list the number of stitches to bind off.) Work to the next marker and repeat until all buttonhole bind offs have been completed.

3. On the next row, work as established to the bound-off stitches, turn the garment, and cast on the same amount of stitches over the bound-off stitches. Turn the garment and work to the next marker. Repeat until all buttonholes have been completed.

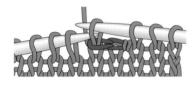

Crochet

Several crochet stitches are commonly used with knitting. We used the chain stitch as a provisional cast on for the socks on page 70. Single crochet is used as an edging for several projects.

CHAIN STITCH

Begin with a slip knot.

1. Wrap yarn over the hook.

2. Draw yarn through the loop on the hook.

3. Repeat steps 1 and 2 until you have the desired length of chain.

SINGLE CROCHET

1. Insert the hook into the knitted fabric. Wrap the yarn around the hook and pull up the loop for a slip stitch.

2. Chain one.

3. Insert the hook into the knitted fabric, yarn over, and pull up the loop.

4. Yarn over and draw through both loops on the hook.

5. Repeat steps 3 and 4 until edging is complete.

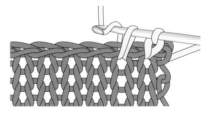

Insert hook into stitch, yarn over hook, pull loop through to front, yarn over hook. Pull loop through both loops on hook.

SLIP STITCH FOR JOINING

1. Insert the hook into the beginning of the crocheted work.

2. Pull up the loop and draw through the stitch on the hook.

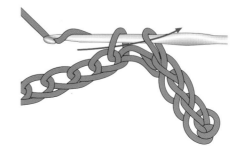

I-Cord

Thanks to Elizabeth Zimmerman, we now use the polite term of "I-cord" for what was once known as "idiot cord." Quite simply, it is a knitted cording that can be used to make a decorative finished edge for your garment.

1. Using double-pointed or 16" circular needles and with the right side of the knitted fabric facing you, pick up and knit one stitch at the desired beginning point of the I-cord.

2. Using the picked-up stitch, cast on three stitches, knit two, knit two together through the back loop, *pick up an additional stitch in the knitted fabric, slide the needle to the opposite end of the work, knit two, knit two together through the back loop. Repeat from * to the desired end of the I-cord. Bind off.

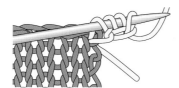

Picked-up stitch and
three cast-on stitches

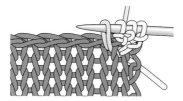

Second stitch picked up

Kitchener Stitch

Kitchener stitch is used for grafting together two pieces of knitted work where a totally flat, seamless look is required. One common use for this method is in sewing together the toe of a sock. A typical seam would make socks uncomfortable to wear as it would add bulk and cause friction where the seam would rub against the inside of the shoe.

1. Hold the stitches to be grafted together on two parallel needles, with the wrong sides of the knitted fabric together.

2. Cut the working yarn, leaving enough yarn to work the desired number of stitches, and thread the yarn tail through a tapestry needle. Insert the needle through the first stitch on the front needle as if to purl, leaving the stitch on the needle.

3. Insert the tapestry needle through the first stitch on the back needle as if to knit, leaving the stitch on the needle. Be sure to pass the yarn under the knitting needles throughout.

4. Insert the tapestry needle through the first stitch on the front needle as if to knit, allowing this stitch to slip off the needle.

5. Insert the tapestry needle through the next stitch on the front needle as if to purl, leaving the stitch on the needle.

6. Insert the tapestry needle through the first stitch on the back needle as if to purl, allowing this stitch to slip off the needle.

7. Insert the tapestry needle through the next stitch on the back needle as if to knit, leaving the stitch on the needle.

8. Repeat steps 4–7 until all stitches have been completed. You may tighten your stitches by gently pulling the yarn from the beginning of the seam to the end.

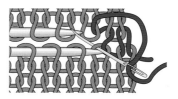

Slip Stitch

Knitwise: (In knitting, it is assumed that all stitches are slipped *purlwise* unless otherwise noted.) Move the first stitch from left-hand needle to right-hand needle as if to knit without working the stitch.

Purlwise: Move the first stitch from left-hand needle to right-hand needle as if to purl without working the stitch.

STRANDING

HAVE YOU EVER WANDERED AROUND A YARN SHOP looking for yarn that is unusual yet beautiful and sturdy? Have you wanted to knit a garment that is unlike any other? Well, if you answered "yes" to either or both of these questions, you have come to the right place. In this section we will introduce you to stranding. Stranding is an easy way to use a selection of different hand-dyed yarns to create your own "signature yarn."

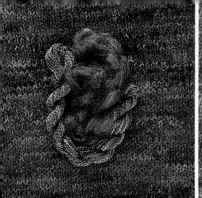   

THE HAND-DYED YARN INDUSTRY has grown considerably over the last few years. As you read this book, you will see that it contains patterns not only for hand-dyed yarn from our company, Wool in the Woods, but also from other businesses that hand dye yarn. Through stranding, you will be able to use all of the new colors and textures available in a remarkably effortless way.

Simply put, in stranding each stitch is made up of multiple strands of yarn. The beauty of stranding is twofold: it is simple to do and you will be able to create the color and texture of your knitted fabric without learning a new stitch.

As you wander around a yarn shop with stranding in mind, there are a couple of things you should contemplate. When selecting hand-dyed yarn to combine for a garment, you should give color, texture, and gauge some consideration. A discussion of the science and art of using color has filled many books. So, for the purpose of this book, our discussion of color will be brief. Basically, there are three easy ways that you can combine colors to create a beautiful garment—shading, color families, and opposing color.

Shading is using variations, or shades, of the same color. For instance, light blue has a lighter density than navy blue. *Color families* are those colors that go together with ease—they are complementary to each other. When describing color families, Anita uses the concept of the color of fire—reds, oranges, yellows. *Opposing colors* are colors that

are opposites and lie next to each other on the color wheel. When Anita talks about opposing color, she refers to them as colors that "fight" because they create energy. When used together, opposing colors draw your eye. That may be why so many professional sports teams use these color combinations for their uniforms. We hope that with the assistance of the color wheel below, you will experiment with color combinations you've never tried before. Or, see "Resources" on page 111 for information on the EK Success company's color wheel. Take this opportunity to "think outside the box" so that you can use opposing colors in a garment that exudes lots of energy and looks fabulous, too!

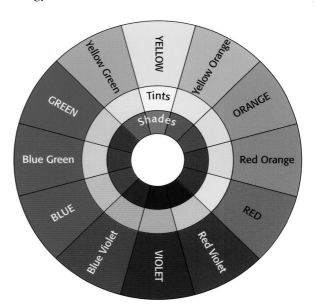

In addition to using stranding to build interesting color combinations, you can also use it to create your own texture. By combining different yarn textures—such as smooth, bouclé, eyelash, cabled, fuzzy, and many others—you can create a variety of textures in the finished piece. When discussing texture, you need to also consider gauge. The gauge of a yarn tells you how long or wide a stitch or group of stitches should be. When you are reading the directions in a pattern, often you will see that the gauge is a simple mathematical equation: a particular number of stitches equals the number of inches or centimeters when knitting with a specified needle size. When you are knitting a garment, it is the gauge that will ensure a proper fit, so as you can see, gauge is incredibly important—especially when you are combining yarns of different weights and textures.

Ordinarily, when shopping for the perfect hand-dyed yarns to knit, you have a pattern in mind for the yarn you are selecting. When you are creating a signature yarn, you will want to approach things a little differently. Create your signature yarn first and then find a pattern that will work well with it. Simply put, you go from gauge to garment. If you create a yarn that is stiff and dense, then you have a perfect yarn for a coat. If you create a yarn that is less dense, then you have a perfect yarn for a sweater or vest. And, if you create a yarn with a significant amount of drape, then you may want to choose a scarf or shawl pattern.

For more information about the gauge and weights of yarns, visit the Craft Yarn Council of America Web site (www.craftyarncouncil.com.) The council has taken on the necessary but thankless task of attempting to standardize many measurements used in knitting—including gauge.

Stranding offers you limitless ways to create a signature yarn. Not only can the color be unique, but the texture and weight can also be combined to produce an exclusive look and feel. Suddenly, your

SWATCH YOUR WAY TO SUCCESS

For stranding, the only way to check to see if you like your color and texture combination is to knit a swatch. Swatching is the most effective way to experiment with hand-dyed yarn combinations. Sometimes the combinations you put together will be lovelier than you imagined. Other combinations, however, will not be what you expected. So, you will want to test your color and texture combinations before you begin knitting your garment. One potential source of yarns to strand into a swatch is your own stash of yarn. Can you think of a more wonderful and creative way to use up your stash? Also, by using your stash to create your signature yarn, your yarns are not sitting idle and taking up space. Just think, the more of your stash you use, the more room you will have for new yarn. So, as Anita likes to say, "Go out on a limb. Try lots of different combinations. Enjoy experimenting!"

yarn store's selection has expanded exponentially with your use of stranding. And, the best part of all is that if you can imagine your ideal yarn, you can now create it.

The four garments in this chapter provide examples of how you can use stranding to create a garment. With Lady of the Lake, Random Ridges, Plain and Pebble Panels, and Flying Solo, you will see how stranding can enrich a garment in a variety of ways.

Lady of the Lake

SKILL LEVEL: EASY ■■□□

 **LADY OF THE LAKE** is a women's pullover crewneck sweater with some beautiful feminine features. By stranding hand-dyed kid mohair yarn with hand-dyed rayon yarn, you can see how a combination of yarns can improve the strength of a weaker yarn. Rayon's two main attributes are that it is shiny and it has beautiful drape. However, if you knit with rayon by itself, your garment will quickly lose its shape and will sag. By stranding a colorful rayon yarn with a stronger yarn like kid mohair, the garment will shimmer like water in a lake and hold its shape.

We knit some notches at the bottom of the sleeves and the sweater to create the illusion of ripples in the lake. Stranding two yarns, Beaded Rayon by Blue Heron Yarns and Feel'n Fuzzy by Wool in the Woods, created this elegant sweater.

Finished Measurements

Bust: 35 (39, 43, 47, 51)"

Length: 21 (21½, 22½, 23½, 24½)"

Materials

A   2 (2, 2, 2, 3) skeins of Blue Heron Beaded Rayon (100% rayon; 525 yds/480 m, 8 oz per skein), color Summer Meadow **3**

B   4 (4, 5, 6, 7) skeins of Wool in the Woods Feel'n Fuzzy (90% kid mohair, 10% nylon; 200 yds/183 m per skein), color Lapis Limits **1**

• Size US 7 (4.5 mm) needles or size required to obtain gauge

• Size US 7 (4.5 mm) 16" circular needles

• Cable needle

• Stitch holders

• Stitch markers

Gauge

18 sts and 24 rows = 4" in St st

Stitch Abbreviations

C2B: Place next stitch on cable needle and hold at back of work. Knit next stitch and then knit stitch from cable needle.

C2F: Place next stitch on cable needle and hold at front of work. Knit next stitch and then knit stitch from cable needle.

Garter Stitch

Knit all rows.

Stockinette Stitch

All RS rows: Knit.

All WS rows: Purl.

NOTE: When using hand-dyed yarn, remember to vary skeins throughout garment to maintain color quality. Hold one strand each of Color A and Color B tog throughout garment.

Back

You will be creating 9 tabs that will be joined after working 14 rows of garter st on each.

Bottom trim: *With A and B held tog, CO 9 (10, 11, 12, 13) sts. Work 14 rows garter st. Cut yarn. Rep from * 8 more times but do not cut yarn last time—81 (90, 99, 108, 117) sts.

Joining row (RS): K8 (9, 10, 11, 12), *C2F, K7 (8, 9, 10, 11); rep from * to last 10 (11, 12, 13, 14) sts, C2F, K8 (9, 10, 11, 12).

Work in St st; dec 1 st at each side every 6th (6th, 6th, 8th, 8th) row 4 times—73 (82, 91, 100, 109) sts. Work until piece measures 7½ (8, 8½, 9, 9)" from bottom trim.

Inc 1 st every 8th row 3 times—79 (88, 97, 106, 115) sts. Work until piece measures 12½ (13, 13½, 14½, 15)".

Armhole shaping: BO 4 sts at each side once. BO 3 sts at each side once. BO 2 sts at each side once. Dec 1 st at each side EOR 2 (3, 3, 3, 3) times. Dec 1 st at each side every 4th row 2 (2, 2, 3, 3) times—53 (60, 69, 76, 85) sts. Work until piece measures 20 (20½, 21½, 22½, 23½)".

Neck shaping: Work 15 (17, 20, 22, 25) sts, place next 23 (26, 29, 32, 35) sts on holder. Join 2nd ball of yarn and work last 15 (17, 20, 22, 25) sts. Working both sides at same time, BO 2 sts at each neck edge once—13 (15, 18, 20, 23) sts. Work until piece measures 21 (21½, 22½, 23½, 24½)". Place shoulder sts on holder.

Front

Work as for back until piece measures 17½ (17½, 18½, 19½, 20½)".

Neck shaping: Work 20 (22, 25, 27, 30) sts, place next 13 (16, 19, 22, 25) sts on holder. Join 2nd ball of yarn and work last 20 (22, 25, 27, 30) sts. Working both sides at same time, BO 3 sts at each neck edge once. BO 2 sts at each neck edge once. Dec 1 st at each neck edge EOR twice—13 (15, 18, 20, 23) sts. Work until piece measures 21 (21½, 22½, 23½, 24½)". Place shoulder sts on holder.

Sleeves (make 2)

*CO 10 (10, 11, 11, 11) sts. Work 14 rows garter st. Cut yarn. Rep from * 2 more times but do not cut yarn last time—30 (30, 33, 33, 33) sts.

Joining row (RS): K9 (9, 10, 10, 10), *C2F, K8 (8, 9, 9, 9); rep from * to last 11 (11, 12, 12, 12) sts, C2F, K9 (9, 10, 10, 10).

Work in St st; inc 1 st at each side EOR 7 (5, 7, 7, 10) times—44 (40, 47, 47, 53) sts. Inc 1 st at each

side every 4th row 15 (18, 17, 17, 16) times—74 (76, 81, 81, 85) sts. Work even until sleeve measures 16 (16½, 17, 17, 17)".

Cap shaping: BO 4 sts at each side once. BO 3 sts at each side once. BO 2 sts at each side once. Dec 1 st at each side EOR 10 (10, 12, 12, 12) times—36 (38, 39, 39, 43) sts. BO 5 sts at each side 3 times. BO remaining 6 (8, 9, 9, 13) sts loosely.

Finishing

Knit shoulder seams tog, using 3-needle BO.

Sew in sleeves.

Sew side seams tog.

Neckband: With RS tog and 16" circular needles, beg at left shoulder seam, PU 20 (21, 21, 22, 23) sts to front holder, K13 (16, 19, 22, 25) sts from holder, PU 20 (21, 21, 22, 23) sts to shoulder seam, PU 6 sts to back holder, K23 (26, 29, 32, 35) sts from holder, and PU 6 sts to shoulder seam; PM and join. Purl 1 rnd. Knit 1 rnd. Purl 1 rnd. BO loosely in knit.

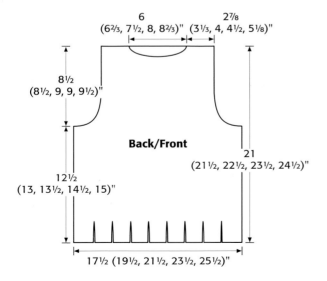

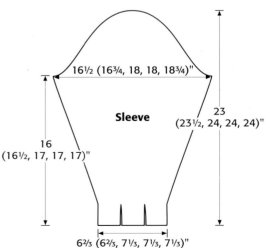

Random Ridges

SKILL LEVEL: EASY ◼◼☐☐

 RANDOM RIDGES is a women's pullover crewneck sweater. For this simple sweater we combined hand-dyed yarns to ensure that the weight of the stranded yarns would be heavy enough to match the gauge of the bulky yarn we chose for the ridges. We wanted to use lace-weight kid mohair for this sweater, but mohair lace yarn is lightweight. Combining it with a sport-weight alpaca created a yarn bulky enough to support the chunky knitted ridges. The main body of the sweater is knit in stockinette stitch, but the ridges—used to enhance the overall colors of the sweater and to add texture—are knit in garter stitch using thick and thin wool.

Stranding two yarns, Heaven by Lorna's Laces and Natural Splendor by Dancing Fibers, created this colorful sweater. The ridges were made with Revelation by Lorna's Laces.

Finished Measurements

Bust: 38 (41, 44, 47, 50)"

Length: 21 (22, 23, 24, 25)"

Materials

A   2 (2, 2, 3, 3) skeins of Lorna's Laces Heaven (90% kid mohair, 10% nylon; 975 yds/892 m, 7 oz per skein), color Bittersweet (**2**)

B   7 (8, 9, 10, 11) skeins of Dancing Fibers Natural Splendor (100% alpaca; 123 yds/113 m, 50 g per skein), color Sherbet (**3**)

C   2 (2, 3, 3, 4) skeins of Lorna's Laces Revelation (100% wool; 125 yds/114 m, 4 oz per skein), color Bittersweet (**5**)

•   Size US 8 (5 mm) needles or size required to obtain gauge

•   Size US 7 (4.5 mm) 16" circular needles

•   Stitch holders

•   Stitch markers

Gauge

16 sts and 21 rows = 4" in St st on larger needles

Seed Stitch

Multiple of 2 + 1 sts

All rows: *K1, P1; rep from * to last st, K1.

Stockinette Stitch

All RS rows: Knit.

All WS rows: Purl.

BODY PATTERN

Rows 1-10: With A and B held tog, work St st.

Row 11 (RS): With C, K31 (34, 37, 40, 43); change to A and B held tog and K45 (48, 51, 54, 57).

Row 12: With A and B held tog, P45 (48, 51, 54, 57); change to C and K31 (34, 37, 40, 43).

Rows 13–22: With A and B held tog, work St st.

Row 23: With A and B held tog, K31 (34, 37, 40, 43); change to C and K45 (48, 51, 54, 57).

Row 24: With C, K45 (48, 51, 54, 57); change to A and B held tog and P31 (34, 37, 40, 43).

Rows 25–34: With A and B held tog, work St st.

Row 35: With C, K12 (15, 18, 21, 24); change to A and B held tog and K52; change to C and K12 (15, 18, 21, 24).

Row 36: With C, K12 (15, 18, 21, 24); change to A and B held tog and P52; change to C and K12 (15, 18, 21, 24).

Rows 37–46: With A and B held tog, work St st.

Row 47: With A and B held tog, K12 (15, 18, 21, 24); change to C and K52; change to A and B held tog and K12 (15, 18, 21, 24).

Row 48: With A and B held tog, P12 (15, 18, 21, 24); change to C and K52; change to A and B held tog and P12 (15, 18, 21, 24).

Rows 49–58: With A and B held tog, work St st.

Row 59: With C, K39 (42, 45, 48, 51); change to A and B held tog and K37 (40, 43, 46, 49).

Row 60: With A and B held tog, P37 (40, 43, 46, 49); change to C and K39 (42, 45, 48, 51).

Rows 61–70: With A and B held tog, work St st.

Row 71: With A and B held tog, K39 (42, 45, 48, 51); change to C and K37 (40, 43, 46, 49).

Row 72: With C, K37 (40, 43, 46, 49); change to A and B held tog and K39 (42, 45, 48, 51).

These 72 rows form body patt.

NOTE: When using hand-dyed yarn, remember to vary skeins throughout garment to maintain color quality.

Back

With A and B held tog and using smaller needles, CO 73 (79, 85, 91, 97) sts. Work 6 rows seed st, inc 3 sts across last WS row—76 (82, 88, 94, 100) sts.

Change to larger needles and work body patt (see "Body Pattern" above) until piece measures 11½ (12, 13, 14, 14½)".

Armhole shaping: Keeping continuity of patt, BO 3 sts at each side once. BO 2 sts at each side once. Dec 1 st at each side EOR 1 (1, 2, 2, 2) time(s)— 64 (70, 74, 80, 86) sts. Work until piece measures 20 (21, 22, 23, 24)".

Neck shaping: Keeping continuity of patt, work 22 (24, 25, 27, 29) sts, place next 20 (22, 24, 26, 28) sts on holder. Join 2nd ball of yarn and work last 22 (24, 25, 27, 29) sts. Working both sides at same time, BO 2 sts at each neck edge once—20 (22, 23, 25, 27) sts.

Work until piece measures 21 (22, 23, 24, 25)". Place shoulder sts on holder.

Front

Work as for back until piece measures 18 (19, 20, 21, 22)".

Neck shaping: Keeping continuity of patt, work 27 (29, 30, 32, 34) sts, place next 10 (12, 14, 16, 18) sts on holder. Join 2nd ball of yarn and work last

27 (29, 30, 32, 34) sts. Working both sides at same time, BO 3 sts at each neck edge once. BO 2 sts at each neck edge once. Dec 1 st at each neck edge EOR twice—20 (22, 23, 25, 27) sts.

Work until piece measures 21 (22, 23, 24, 25)". Place shoulder sts on holder.

Sleeves (make 2)

With A and B held tog and smaller needles, CO 33 (35, 35, 35, 37) sts. Work seed st as for back, inc 3 sts across last WS row—36 (38, 38, 38, 40) sts.

Change to larger needles and work sleeve patt (see "Sleeve Pattern" below) until piece measures 16½ (17, 17½, 18, 18½)", inc 1 st at each side every 4th row 20 times—76 (78, 78, 78, 80) sts.

Cap shaping: Keeping continuity of patt, BO 3 sts at each side once. BO 2 sts at each side once. Dec 1 st at each side EOR 1 (1, 2, 2, 2) time(s)—64 (66, 64, 64, 66) sts. BO rem sts loosely.

SLEEVE PATTERN

NOTE: The sleeve pattern is worked over 34 sts set off by markers. When working the patt, use established yarn outside markers. For example, to work row 11, begin row with C, knit to marker, K14 with C, change to A and B held tog, K20, knit to end of row with A and B held tog.

Rows 1 (RS)–10: With A and B held tog, work St st, placing markers on either side of center 34 sts.

Row 11: With C, K14; change to A and B held tog, K20.

Row 12: With A and B held tog, P20; change to C, K14.

Rows 13–22: With A and B held tog, work St st.

Row 23: With A and B held tog, K18; change to C, K16.

Row 24: With C, K16; change to A and B held tog, P18.

Rows 25–34: With A and B held tog, work St st.

Row 35: With C, K10; change to A and B held tog, K24.

Row 36: With A and B held tog, P24; change to C, K10.

Rows 37–46: With A and B held tog, work St st.

Row 47: With A and B held tog, K12; change to C, K22.

Row 48: With C, K22; change to A and B held tog, P12.

These 48 rows form patt.

Finishing

Knit shoulder seams tog, using 3-needle BO.

Sew in sleeves.

Sew side seams tog.

Neckband: With RS tog, A and B held tog, and 16" circular needles, beg at left shoulder seam, PU 20 sts to front holder, K10 (12, 14, 16, 18) sts from holder. PU 20 sts to shoulder seam, PU 5 sts to back holder, K20 (22, 24, 26, 28) sts from holder, PU 5 sts to shoulder seam; PM and join. Work seed st for 5 rnds as foll:

Rnds 1, 3, and 5: *K1, P1; rep from * around.

Rnds 2, and 4: *P1, K1; rep from * around.

BO loosely in seed st.

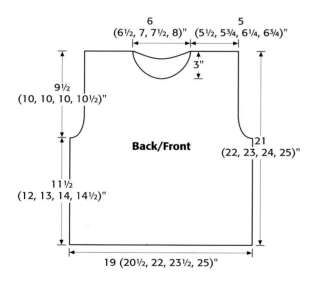

6
(6½, 7, 7½, 8)" 5 (5½, 5¾, 6¼, 6¾)"

3"

9½
(10, 10, 10, 10½)"

Back/Front

21 (22, 23, 24, 25)"

11½
(12, 13, 14, 14½)"

19 (20½, 22, 23½, 25)"

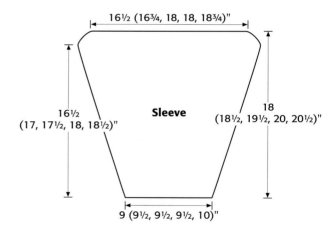

16½ (16¾, 18, 18, 18¾)"

16½
(17, 17½, 18, 18½)"

Sleeve

18
(18½, 19½, 20, 20½)"

9 (9½, 9½, 9½, 10)"

Plain and Pebble Panels

PLAIN AND PEBBLE PANELS is a women's pullover crewneck sweater. The impetus for this lightweight sweater's combination of color and texture was some yarn in our stash that we really liked but had not yet figured out how to use in a garment. This yarn, Sapphire Wrap, is a fine cotton-polyester wrap. So, we spent some creative time making swatches by stranding different hand-dyed yarns with the wrap. Once we found our desired gauge, we designed this sweater.

The wrap was stranded with a smooth wool to knit half of the sweater, and a bumpy yarn to knit the other half. Thus, the smooth side created the "plain" half of the sweater and the bumpy side created the "pebble" side of the sweater. Three yarns created this playful sweater: Cherub, Wilkson, and Sapphire Wrap by Wool in the Woods.

Finished Measurements

Bust: 40 (44, 48, 52)"

Length: 21 (21, 23, 25)"

Materials

A   4 (4, 5, 6) skeins of Wool in the Woods Cherub (100% wool; 200 yds/183 m per skein), color H20 ⬤❶⬤

B   4 (4, 5, 6) skeins of Wool in the Woods Wilkson (93% wool, 7% nylon; 200 yds/183 m per skein), color H20 ⬤❷⬤

C   6 (6, 7, 8) skeins of Wool in the Woods Sapphire Wrap (cotton/acrylic blend; 200 yds/183 m per skein), color H20

- Size US 7 (4.5 mm) needles or size required to obtain gauge

- Size F (3.75 mm) crochet hook

- Stitch holders

Gauge

20 sts and 30 rows = 4" in St st with A and C held tog and B and C held tog

Stockinette Stitch

All RS rows: Knit.

All WS rows: Purl.

edge 1 (1, 1, 2) time(s). BO 2 sts at each neck edge 1 (1, 2, 1) time(s). Dec 1 st at each neck edge EOR 3 (4, 4, 4) times—33 (37, 40, 44) sts.

Work until panels measure 21 (21, 23, 25)". Place shoulder sts on holder.

Sleeves (make 2 panels with A and C; make 2 panels with B and C)

CO 19 (19, 19, 21) sts for each panel. Knit 1 row (WS).

Work sleeve panels in St st, inc 1 st at each side every 6th row 15 (16, 16, 16) times—49 (51, 51, 53) sts.

Work even until sleeve panels measure 17 (17½, 18, 18½)". BO sts loosely.

NOTE: When using hand-dyed yarn, remember to vary skeins throughout garment to maintain color quality.

Back (work 2 panels tog)

With B and C held tog, use a long-tail CO (see page 16) to CO 50 (55, 60, 65) sts. With A and a 2nd ball of C, CO 50 (55, 60, 65) sts. Count this as row 1.

Knit 1 row (WS).

Knit next row and then work both panels in St st until panels measure 20 (20, 22, 24)".

Neck shaping: BO 15 (16, 18, 19) sts at each neck edge once. BO 2 sts at each neck edge once—33 (37, 40, 44) sts.

Work until panels measure 21 (21, 23, 25)". Place shoulder sts on holder.

Front (work panels tog)

Work as for back until panels measure 18 (18, 20, 22)".

Neck shaping: BO 5 sts at each neck edge once. BO 4 sts at each neck edge once. BO 3 sts at each neck

Finishing

All seams will be finished to the outside of the garment using A.

With WS tog, knit shoulder seams tog, using 3-needle BO. Be sure to place A-C texture next to B-C texture when joining sleeve to body.

With one A-C panel and one B-C panel held WS tog, use crochet hook to slip-stitch sleeve seam (see "Slip Stitch for Joining" on page 17). Rep for other sleeve.

Measure 9½ (10, 10, 10½)" from shoulder seam on front and back, pin sleeve in place between these markings, and slip-st sleeve to body.

With WS tog, use a crochet hook to slip-st side seams.

Sleeve, neck, and bottom trim: With A and C held tog, sc around each opening (see "Single Crochet" on page 17).

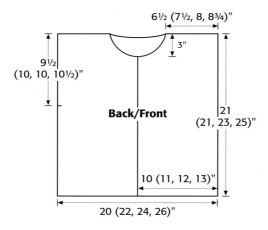

6½ (7½, 8, 8¾)"

3"

9½
(10, 10, 10½)"

Back/Front

21
(21, 23, 25)"

10 (11, 12, 13)"

20 (22, 24, 26)"

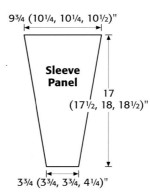

9¾ (10¼, 10¼, 10½)"

Sleeve Panel

17
(17½, 18, 18½)"

3¾ (3¾, 3¾, 4¼)"

Flying Solo

SKILL LEVEL: EXPERIENCED ◼◼◼◻

FLYING SOLO is a women's V-neck cardigan. This sweater is a quick knit, because it's knit with bulky yarn on big needles. But, please do not be fooled by the word "quick." We would not classify this sweater as easy to knit because of its unusual construction. The sleeves are worked by casting on stitches to the sweater fronts and back. An added design element of this cardigan is that there are seams on top of the arms. The advantage of this sleeve construction is that there is no bulging of knitted fabric at the back of a woman's shoulder. This gorgeous sweater moves with the body and creates a sleek line. Made by stranding three yarns—Dusty Road, Feel'n Fuzzy, and Sparkle, all by Wool in the Woods—this sweater exemplifies all of the virtues of stranding with hand-dyed yarn. We have found that freshwater-pearl buttons with their variation in color and texture, provide a lovely complement to the hand-dyed yarn.

Finished Measurements

Bust: 40 (43½, 46½, 50)"

Length: 21½ (23, 24, 24½)"

Materials

A   4 (5, 5, 6) skeins of Wool in the Woods Dusty Road (mohair blend; 200 yds/183 m per skein), color Lottery (**5**)

B   4 (5, 5, 6) skeins of Wool in the Woods Feel'n Fuzzy (90% mohair, 10% nylon; 200 yds/183 m per skein), color Denim Blue (**1**)

C   4 (5, 5, 6) skeins of Wool in the Woods Sparkle (100% rayon; 200 yds/183 m per skein), color Birch Run (**2**)

• Size US 10½ (6.5 mm) 16" and 36" circular needles or size required to obtain gauge

• Cable needle

• 5 buttons, ⅞" diameter

• Stitch holders

• Split-ring stitch markers

Gauge

12 sts and 16 rows = 4" in St st

Stockinette Stitch

All RS rows: Knit.

All WS rows: Purl.

NOTE: Hold 1 strand each of Colors A, B, and C tog throughout garment. When using hand-dyed yarn, remember to vary skeins throughout garment to maintain color quality.

Body

With 36" circular needles, CO 112 (122, 132, 142) sts.

Work in St st, inc 1 st at each front edge EOR 4 times—120 (130, 140, 150) sts.

Next row (RS): K30 (33, 35, 38), PM, K60 (64, 70, 74), PM, K30 (33, 35, 38).

Work in St st until piece measures 3½ (4, 4½, 4½)".

Dec Row (RS): Knit to 2 sts before first marker, K2tog, sl marker, ssk, knit to 2 sts before 2nd marker, K2tog, sl marker, ssk, knit to end of row.

Work dec row—116 (126, 136, 146) sts.

Work in St st until piece measure 5 (5½, 6, 6)".

Work dec row as before—112 (122, 132, 142) sts.

Work in St st until piece measures 6 (6½, 7, 7)".

Work dec row as before—108 (118, 128, 138) sts.

Work in St st until piece measures 7½ (8, 8½, 8½)".

Inc Row (RS): Knit to 1 st before first marker, inc 1 st in st below next st on needle, K1, sl marker, K1, inc 1 st in st below st just worked, knit to 1 st before 2nd marker, inc 1 st in st below next st on needle, K1, sl marker, K1, inc 1 st in st below st just worked, knit to end of row.

Work inc row—112 (122, 132, 142) sts.

Work in St st until piece measures 9 (9½, 10, 10)".

Work inc row—116 (126, 136, 146) sts.

Work in St st until piece measures 10½ (11, 11½, 11½)".

Work inc row —120 (130, 140, 150) sts.

Work in St st until piece measures 12 (13, 14, 14)", ending on a WS row.

Divide for fronts and back: Pass first 30 (33, 35, 38) sts to needle with second 30 (33, 35, 38) sts, place back 60 (64, 70, 74) sts on holder.

Fronts

Work the fronts and sleeves at the same time. Although it may seem awkward, you will be casting on sts for sleeves and working the armhole dec at the same time.

Mark first st at armhole edges by placing a split-ring marker on the individual stitch, not on the needle. CO 9 sts at each armhole edge once. CO 8 sts at each armhole edge once. CO 7 sts at each armhole edge once. CO 6 sts at each armhole edge once. CO 5 sts at each armhole edge once. CO 4 sts at each armhole edge once. CO 3 sts at each armhole edge 4 times. (**NOTE:** All CO stitches are added at end

of row as you approach sleeve/shoulder side. That means you'll CO sts to right front on knit rows and CO sts to left front on purl rows.) AT SAME TIME, work dec rows for armhole 6 times, as foll:

Left front, row 1 (RS): Knit to marked st, place marked st on cable needle, hold at front of work, K2tog, K1 from cable needle, knit to end.

Right front, row 1 (RS): Knit to 2 sts before marked st, place 2 sts on cable needle, hold at back of work, K1, ssk from cable needle, knit to end.

Row 2: Purl 75 (78, 80, 83) sts.

Rep rows 1 and 2 six times.

Cont moving sts as est, working next 2 rows 4 times:

Left front, row 1 (RS): Knit to marked st, place marked st on cable needle, hold at front of work, K1, K1 from cable needle, knit to end.

Right front, row 1 (RS): Knit to 1 st before marked st, place st on cable needle, hold at back of work, K1, K1 from cable needle, knit to end.

Row 2: Purl—75 (78, 80, 83) sts.

> At this time, the total number of sleeve sts is complete. You will continue to dec at cable and inc at sleeve cuff to continue the shaping, but the total number of stitches will remain the same.

Left front, row 1 (RS): Inc 1 st in first sleeve st, knit to 2 sts before marked st, place 2 sts on cable needle, hold at back of work, K1, K2tog from cable needle, knit to end.

Right front, row 1 (RS): Knit to marked st, place st on cable needle, hold at front of work, ssk, K1 from cable needle, knit to last st, inc 1 st in last st.

Row 2: Purl—75 (78, 80, 83) sts.

Work these 2 rows until piece measures 17½ (18, 18½, 19)".

Neck shaping: Cont to work last 2 rows; AT SAME TIME dec 1 st at each neck edge EOR 9 (10, 10, 11) time(s)—66 (68, 70, 72) sts. Cont as est until piece measures 21½ (23, 24, 24½)". Place sts on holder or spare circular needle.

Back

Place 60 (64, 70, 74) sts from holder on needle for back. Mark first st at armhole edges. CO sleeve sts as for fronts. AT SAME TIME, work dec rows for armhole 6 times as foll:

Row 1 (RS): Knit to first marked st, place marked st on cable needle, hold at front of work, K2tog, K1 from cable needle, knit to 2 sts before second marked st, place 2 sts on cable needle, hold at back of work, K1, ssk from cable needle, knit to end.

Row 2: Purl 150 (154, 160, 164) sts.

Cont moving sts as est, working next 2 rows 4 times:

Row 1 (RS): Knit to first marked st, place marked st on cable needle, hold at front of work, K1, K1 from cable needle, knit to 1 st before second marked st, place st on cable needle, hold at back of work, K1, K1 from cable needle, knit to end.

Row 2: Purl—150 (154, 160, 164) sts.

> At this time, the total number of sleeve sts is complete. You will continue to dec at cable and inc at sleeve cuff for shaping, but the total number of sts will not change.

Work the foll 2 rows until piece measures 20½ (22, 23, 23½)":

Row 1 (RS): Inc 1 st in first sleeve st, knit to 2 sts before first marked st, place 2 sts on cable needle, hold at back of work, K1, K2tog from cable needle, knit to second marked st, place st on cable needle, hold at front of work, ssk, K1 from cable needle, knit to last st, inc 1 in last st.

Row 2: Purl.

Neck shaping: Cont as est. Work 68 (70, 72, 74) sts. BO 14 (14, 16, 16) sts. Work last 68 (70, 72, 74) sts. BO 2 sts at each neck edge once—66 (68, 70, 72) sts. Place sts on holder.

Finishing

Knit shoulder and upper sleeve seams tog, WS tog.

Sew sleeve underarm seams.

Mark 5 evenly spaced buttonholes on right front between bottom inc and V-neck opening.

Body band: With RS tog, beg at right bottom. PU 1 st in each knit st to front edge. PU 6 sts through inc, K1, *CO 2 sts at marker, skip 2, PU 11 (11, 12, 12) sts to next marker; rep from * to last buttonhole, CO 2 sts at marker, skip 2. PU 16 (17, 17, 18) sts to shoulder seam, PU 6 sts to back holder, K14 sts from holder, PU 6 sts to shoulder seam, PU 16 (17, 17, 18) sts to V-neck, PU 55 (55, 59, 59) sts to inc, PU 6 sts through inc, PU 1 st in each knit st to left side seam; PM and join. Purl 2 rows. BO in purl.

Sleeve band: With RS tog, beg at underarm, use the 16" circular needles to PU 33 (35, 35, 37) sts around; PM and join. Purl 2 rows. BO in purl.

Sew buttons to left front.

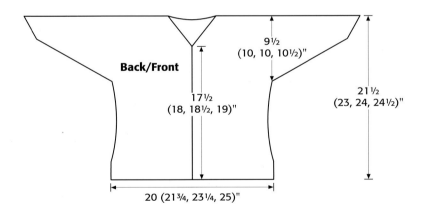

Back/Front

9½ (10, 10, 10½)"

17½ (18, 18½, 19)"

21½ (23, 24, 24½)"

20 (21¾, 23¼, 25)"

KNIT AND PURL

KNITTING AND PURLING ARE THE FOUNDATION of all other knitting stitches. Together these two simple stitches are tried-and-true and offer the added bonus of creating two distinct textures: the smooth stockinette stitch, with all knitting stitches on the right side of the garment, and the bumpy reverse stockinette stitch, with all purl stitches on the right side. When you mix up the combination of knit and purl stitches in a garment, you can create a wide array of textured knitting patterns.

ANITA DESCRIBES a textured knitting pattern as a sequence of knit and purl stitches followed over and over again to form a particular pattern. The stitch itself creates depth, since there appears to be a bump wherever there are purl stitches. The bumps are not above the plane of the knitted fabric; they are merely an impression created by the way the stitch is formed. They give the appearance of depth in the knitting, just as the natural color variations in hand-dyed yarn give the appearance of depth. When you combine the subtle shading differences in hand-dyed yarn with textured knitting, the result is a garment that is as rich and dimensional as an impressionist painting.

The best way to use these two color-enhancing ideas—textured knitting and hand-dyed yarn—is to search for a pattern that is simple and repetitive. For instance, a great pattern to use would be a rib pattern. It is best to avoid patterns with pictorial designs like the alphabet, trees, flowers, and animals. When combining knit and purl stitches and hand-dyed yarn, you are not knitting the pattern for the pattern's sake; the pattern itself isn't what makes the statement. You are attempting to show off the depth of the yarn color to make a unique and striking garment.

The four garments in this chapter illustrate how elegantly simple stitches, when combined with just one multicolored or monocolored hand-dyed yarn, can make a spectacular garment that showcases the yarn's spectrum of colors. Cream of the Crop, Ribbed Elegance, Steppin' Out, and Is It a Vest? Is It a Shawl? are all keen examples of how the simplicity of a stitch, combined with the depth of color of hand-dyed yarn, can produce garments that are works of art.

Cream of the Crop

 **CREAM OF THE CROP** is a women's crewneck pullover. This sweater was knit with a hand-dyed monocolored yarn. Though many people feel the inherent beauty of hand-dyed yarn is in the variegated colors, some knitters like to knit a single-colored garment. By knitting a garment using a patterned stitch with a monocolored hand-dyed yarn, you still enjoy all of the other benefits of using hand-dyed yarn—intense, rich color and incredible fibers. Monocolored hand-dyed yarn displays the subtle nuances of one color, bringing out all of the luxurious hues of a single color.

This sweater, though it appears to be complicated, is actually a combination of knit and purl stitches worked in different patterns. The purl stitch travels diagonally to create diamonds on the surface of the sweater front and back. The sleeves are worked in the bobble rib pattern. Knitting and purling one yarn—Blue Sky Worsted by Blue Sky Alpacas, Inc.—created this remarkable sweater.

Finished Measurements

Bust: 38½ (43, 47½, 52)"

Length: 21 (22, 23, 24)"

Materials

- 8 (10, 12, 14) skeins of Blue Sky Alpacas Blue Sky Worsted (50% alpaca, 50% merino; 100 yds/91 m, 100 g per skein), color Butter 🌀**4**

- Size US 10 (6 mm) needles or size required to obtain gauge

- Stitch holders

- Stitch markers

Gauge

14 sts and 19 rows = 4" in body patt

Bobble Rib Pattern

Multiple of 8 + 3 sts

Row 1 (RS): K3, *P2, [P1, K1] twice into next st, pass first 3 of these sts, one at a time, over 4th st, P2, K3; rep from * to end.

Rows 2 and 4: P3, *K2, P1, K2, P3; rep from * to end.

Row 3: K3, *P2, K1, P2, K3; rep from * to end.

These 4 rows form rib patt.

Body Pattern

Multiple of 8 + 3 sts

Row 1 (RS): K1, *P1, K7; rep from * to last 2 sts, P1, K1.

Rows 2 and 8: K1, *P1, K1, P5, K1; rep from * to last 2 sts, P1, K1.

Rows 3 and 7: K1, *K2, P1, K3, P1, K1; rep from * to last 2 sts, K2.

Rows 4 and 6: K1, *P3, K1, P1, K1, P2; rep from * to last 2 sts, P1, K1.

Row 5: K1, *K4, P1, K3; rep from * to last 2 sts, K2.

These 8 rows form body patt.

NOTE: When using hand-dyed yarn, remember to vary skeins throughout garment to maintain color quality.

Back

Using a long-tail CO (see page 16), CO 67 (75, 83, 91) sts. Count the CO row as row 1.

Work in bobble rib patt for 5", beg with row 2 and ending with row 2 or 4. Work in body patt until piece measures 12 (13, 13½, 14)".

Armhole shaping: Keeping continuity of patt, BO 3 sts at each side once. BO 2 sts at each side once. Dec 1 st at each side EOR 3 (3, 4, 4) times—51 (59, 65, 73) sts.

Work until piece measures 20 (21, 22, 23)".

Neck shaping: Keeping continuity of patt, work 17 (20, 22, 25) sts, place next 17 (19, 21, 23) sts on holder. Join 2nd ball of yarn and work last 17 (20, 22, 25) sts. Working both sides at same time, BO 2 sts at each neck edge once—15 (18, 20, 23) sts.

Work until piece measures 21 (22, 23, 24)". Place shoulder sts on holder.

Front

Work as for back until piece measures 17 (18, 19, 20)".

Neck shaping: Keeping continuity of patt, work 20 (23, 25, 28) sts, place next 11 (13, 15, 17) sts on holder. Join 2nd ball of yarn and work last 20 (23, 25, 28) sts. Working both sides at same time, BO 2 sts at each neck edge once. Dec 1 st at each neck edge EOR 3 times—15 (18, 20, 23) sts.

Work until piece measures 21 (22, 23, 24)". Place shoulder sts on holder.

Sleeves (make 2)

CO 27 (27, 35, 35) sts. Work in bobble rib patt, inc 1 st at each side every 6th row 3 (3, 4, 4) times—33 (33, 43, 43) sts.

Inc 1 st at each side every 4th row 11 times—55 (55, 65, 65) sts.

Inc 1 st at each side EOR 4 (4, 2, 2) times—63 (63, 69, 69) sts.

Work even until sleeve measures 16 (17, 17½, 18)".

Cap shaping: Keeping continuity of patt, BO 3 sts at each side once. BO 2 sts at each side once. Dec 1 st at each side EOR 10 times—33 (33, 39, 39) sts. BO 3 sts at each side 3 times. BO remaining 15 (15, 21, 21) sts loosely.

When working in a particular pattern and increasing or decreasing stitches at the same time, you may not always have enough stitches to work a particular part of the pattern at each end of your work. In this case, you will not always have enough stitches at the end of the sleeves to make a bobble. Simply purl the stitches until you have enough stitches to make a bobble.

Finishing

Knit shoulder seams tog, using 3-needle BO.

Sew in sleeves.

Sew side seams tog.

Neckband: With RS tog, beg at left shoulder seam, PU 18 (20, 22, 24) sts to front holder, K11 (13, 15, 17) sts from holder, PU 18 (20, 22, 24) sts to shoulder seam, PU 4 sts to back holder, K17 (19, 21, 23) sts from holder, PU 4 sts to shoulder seam; PM and join—72 (80, 88, 92) sts. Work ribbing as foll:

> **Rnds 1, 2, and 4:** *P2, K1, P2, K3; rep from * around.

> **Rnd 3:** P2, [P1, K1] twice into next st, pass first 3 of these sts, one at a time, over 4th st, P2, K3; rep from * around.

BO in ribbing.

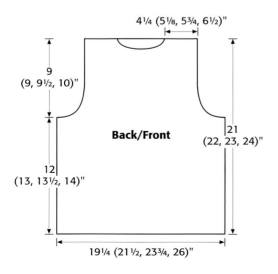

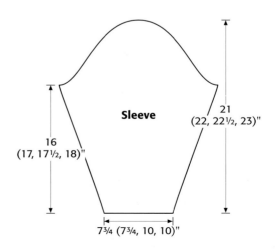

Ribbed Elegance

SKILL LEVEL: INTERMEDIATE ■■■▢

 RIBBED ELEGANCE is a women's cardigan knit with one multicolored hand-dyed yarn. It boldly illustrates how different stitches can show all of the colors in hand-dyed yarn. This sweater features knit and purl stitches in a ribbing pattern. The stitch pattern enriches the color in this sweater because light hits the yarn at three different levels. The contrast between the highest stitches and the shadows of the lowest ones shows off the multicolored yarn to its best advantage.

Knitting and purling one yarn, Mountain Goat by Mountain Colors, created this spectacular ribbed cardigan.

Finished Measurements

Bust: 39½ (41¼, 43½, 45¼, 47½)"

Length: 22 (23, 24, 25, 25)"

Materials

- 6 (6, 7, 8, 8) skeins of Mountain Colors Mountain Goat (55% mohair, 45% wool; 230 yds/210 m, 100 g per skein), color Ruby River 🄸

- Size US 6 (4 mm) needles or size required to obtain gauge

- Size US 6 (4 mm) double-pointed or 16" circular needles

- 3 clasps

- Stitch holders

Gauge

20 sts and 32 rows = 4" in patt

To swatch, work 23 sts in patt but measure only 20 sts.

Rib Pattern

Rows 1 and 3 (RS): P3 (0, 3, 0, 3), K3, *P3, K1, P3, K3; rep from * to last 3 (0, 3, 0, 3) sts, P3 (0, 3, 0, 3) sts.

Row 2: K3 (0, 3, 0, 3), P3, *K3, P1, K3, P3; rep from * to last 3 (0, 3, 0, 3) sts, K3 (0, 3, 0, 3) sts.

Row 4: Knit.

NOTE: When using hand-dyed yarn, remember to vary skeins throughout garment to maintain color quality.

Back

CO 99 (103, 109, 113, 119) sts. Work in rib patt until piece measures 13 (13½, 14½, 15, 15)", ending with WS row.

Armhole shaping: Keeping continuity of patt, BO 3 sts at each armhole edge once. BO 2 sts at each armhole edge 1 (1, 1, 2, 2) time(s). Dec 1 st at each armhole edge EOR 5 (5, 6, 5, 5) times—79 (83, 87, 89, 95) sts. Work until piece measures 21 (22, 23, 24, 24)".

Neck shaping: Keeping continuity of patt, work 26 (27, 28, 29, 31) sts, place next 27 (29, 31, 31, 33) sts on holder. Join 2nd ball of yarn and work last 26 (27, 28, 29, 31) sts. Working both sides at same time, BO 2 sts at each neck edge once—24 (25, 26, 27, 29) sts. Work until piece measures 22 (23, 24, 25, 25)". Place shoulder sts on holder.

Fronts (work both pieces at same time)

CO 49 (53, 56, 59, 63) sts for each front. Work in patt as foll until pieces measure 13 (13½, 14½, 15, 15)", ending with WS row.

LEFT FRONT

Row 1 (RS): P3 (0, 3, 0, 3), K3, * P3, K1, P3, K3; rep from * to last 3 (0, 0, 6, 7) sts, P3 (0, 0, 3, 3), K0 (0, 0, 1, 1), P0 (0, 0, 2, 3).

Row 2: K0 (0, 0, 2, 3), P0 (0, 0, 1, 1), K3 (0, 0, 3, 3), * P3, K3, P1, K3; rep from * to last 6 (3, 6, 3, 6) sts, P3, K3 (0, 3, 0, 3).

Row 3: Work row 1.

Row 4: Knit.

RIGHT FRONT

Row 1 (RS): P0 (0, 0, 2, 3), K0 (0, 0, 1, 1), P3 (0, 0, 3, 3), *K3, P3, K1, P3; rep from * to last 6 (3, 6, 3, 6) sts, K3, P3 (0, 3, 0, 3).

Row 2: K3 (0, 3, 0, 3), P3, *K3, P1, K3, P3; rep from * to last 3 (0, 0, 6, 7) sts, K3 (0, 0, 3, 3), P0 (0, 0, 1, 1), K0 (0, 0, 2, 3).

Row 3: Work row 1.

Row 4: Knit.

ARMHOLE AND NECK SHAPING

Keeping continuity of patt, work armhole shaping as for back. AT SAME TIME, when pieces measure 13½ (14½, 15½, 16½, 16½)", dec 1 st at each neck edge EOR 7 (8, 10, 12, 14) times—32 (35, 35, 35, 37) sts. Dec 1 st at each neck edge every 4th row 8 (10, 9, 8, 8) times—24 (25, 26, 27, 29) sts. Work in patt until pieces measure 22 (23, 24, 25, 25)".

Sleeves (make 2)

CO 43 sts. Keeping continuity of patt, inc 1 st at each side EOR 0 (0, 4, 4, 4) times. Inc 1 st at each side every 4th row 24 (24, 22, 24, 24) times—91 (91, 95, 99, 99) sts. Work even until sleeve measures 15 (15½, 16, 16½, 17)".

Cap shaping: BO 3 sts at each side once. BO 2 sts at each side 1 (1, 1, 2, 2) time(s). Dec 1 st at each side EOR 14 (14, 16, 16, 16) times—53 sts. BO 3 sts at each side 4 times. BO remaining 29 sts loosely.

Finishing

Knit shoulder seams tog, using 3-needle BO.

Sew side seams tog.

Work attached I-cord edging around fronts as foll: With double-pointed or 16" circular needles, PU 1 st in bottom right front. CO 3 sts using the picked-up st. K2, K2tog tbl. PU 1 st on right front. Slide needle to other end, K2, K2tog tbl. Cont in this manner to end (see page 18 for illustration of attached I-cord).

Sew clasps to left and right fronts.

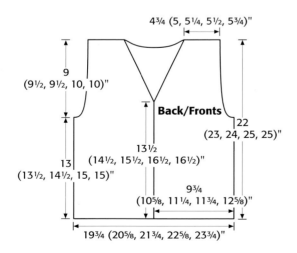

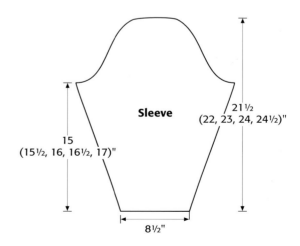

Steppin' Out

SKILL LEVEL: EASY ◖■□◗

 STEPPIN' OUT is a men's vest knit with one multicolored hand-dyed yarn. This vest is a perfect example of how colors in hand-dyed yarn move through a garment even though you are knitting the same stitch throughout. On the left vest front, you can see that the color changes from a horizontal design to a vertical pattern toward the shoulder, simply because the number of stitches in a row changes as the shoulder is shaped. This sweater was worked in a semi-rib pattern, which was selected specifically because the furrows and shadows further act to add depth and enrich the colors of the vest. To finish the vest, the edges are knit in stockinette stitch, creating a rolled edge around the vest. Knitting and purling one yarn, Cyclone by Wool in the Woods, created this colorful yet subdued vest.

Finished Measurements

Chest: 40½ (43½, 47, 50, 53)"

Length: 23 (24, 25, 25, 26)"

Materials

- 5 (6, 7, 7, 8) skeins of Wool in the Woods Cyclone (100% wool; 200 yds/183 m per skein), color Uptown **4**

- Size US 8 (5 mm) needles or size required to obtain gauge

- Size US 7 (4.5 mm) needles

- Size US 7 (4.5 mm) 16" circular needles

- 5 buttons, ⅞" diameter

- Stitch holders

- Stitch markers

Gauge

20 sts and 24 rows = 4" in patt on larger needles

Rib Pattern

Multiples of 4 + 1 sts

Row 1 (RS): P1, *K3, P1; rep from * to end.

Row 2: K2, P1, *K3, P1; rep from * to last 2 sts, K2.

Stockinette Stitch

All RS rows: Knit.

All WS rows: Purl.

NOTE: When using hand-dyed yarn, remember to vary skeins throughout garment to maintain color quality.

Back

With smaller needles, CO 101 (109, 117, 125, 133) sts. Work 8 rows St st.

Change to larger needles and work rib patt until piece measures 13 (14, 14½, 14½, 15)", ending with WS row.

Armhole shaping: Keeping continuity of patt, BO 3 sts at each armhole edge twice. BO 2 sts at each armhole edge 1 (1, 2, 2, 2) time(s). Dec 1 st at each armhole edge EOR 4 (4, 3, 3, 4) times—77 (85, 91, 99, 105) sts. Work until piece measures 22 (23, 24, 24, 25)".

Neck shaping: Keeping continuity of patt, work 24 (27, 29, 32, 34) sts, place next 29 (31, 33, 35, 37) sts on holder. Join 2nd ball of yarn and work last 24 (27, 29, 32, 34) sts. Working both sides at same time, BO 2 sts at each neck edge once—22 (25, 27, 30, 32) sts. Work until piece measures 23 (24, 25, 25, 26)". Place shoulder sts on holder.

Fronts (work both pieces at same time)

With smaller needles, CO 53 (57, 61, 65, 69) sts for each front. Work in patt as for back until pieces measure 13 (14, 14½, 14½, 15)", ending with WS row.

Armhole and neck shaping: Keeping continuity of patt, work armhole shaping as for back. AT SAME TIME, when piece measures 15 (16, 16½, 16½,

17)", dec 1 st at each neck edge EOR 19 (20, 21, 22, 23) times—22 (25, 27, 30, 32) sts. Work in patt until pieces measure 23 (24, 25, 25, 26)".

Finishing

Knit shoulder seams tog, using 3-needle BO.

Sew side seams tog.

Armhole bands: With 16" circular needles and RS tog, PU 102 (102, 104, 104, 106) sts around armhole; PM and join. Knit 7 rows. BO loosely in knit.

Front and neckbands: Mark 5 buttonholes evenly beg at V-neck on left front and ending at 12" below first buttonhole. (This will allow for vent at bottom.) With circular needles and RS tog, PU 67 (70, 72, 72, 75) sts to V-neck, PU 38 (38, 40, 40, 42) sts to shoulder seam, PU 5 sts to back holder, K29 (31, 33, 35, 37) sts from back holder, PU 5 sts to shoulder seam, PU 38 (38, 40, 40, 42) sts to front V-neck, PU 2 sts. *Turn work, CO 3 sts, turn work, skip 3; PU 11 sts to next marker; rep from * to last buttonhole, turn work, CO 3 sts, turn work, skip 3; PU 6 (9, 11, 11, 15) sts to bottom. Work St st for 7 rows, inc 2 sts across back neck edge on each RS row. BO loosely in knit.

Sew buttons to right front.

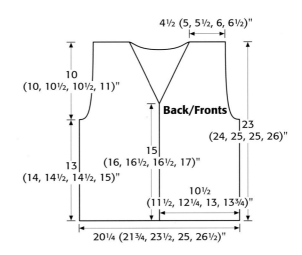

Is It a Vest? Is It a Shawl?

SKILL LEVEL: BEGINNER ⬤▢▢▢

IS IT A VEST? IS IT A SHAWL? is a women's outer garment knit with one multicolored, hand-dyed yarn using stockinette and seed stitches. It is another clear example of how the hand-dyed yarn does the work of moving the color throughout your project. This garment is essentially a knitted rectangle, but because of the way it drapes when worn on the body, the colors fall differently than you might expect. The color changes on the flaps in the front appear to happen horizontally while the color shifts on the back are vertical. Knitting and purling one yarn, Sophie by Wool in the Woods, created this truly unique garment.

Finished Measurements

Back (from shoulder to shoulder): 16 (17, 18, 19)"

Length: 25¾ (26¾, 27¾, 27¾)"

To determine which size to knit, have a friend measure you from shoulder tip to shoulder tip.

Materials

- 5 (5, 6, 6) skeins of Wool in the Woods Sophie (50% llama, 50% wool; 200 yds/183 m per skein), color Lottery (4)

- Size US 9 (5.5 mm) needles or size required to obtain gauge

- Size H (5 mm) crochet hook

- 1 shawl pin by Skacel Collection, Inc. (see "Resources" on page 111)

- Stitch markers

Gauge

16 sts and 22 rows = 4" in St st

Seed Stitch

All rows: *K1, P1; rep from * to last st, K1.

Stockinette Stitch

All RS rows: Knit.

All WS rows: Purl.

To reduce the chance of yarn ends popping out, felt the joinings in this garment. To do so, fray the yarn on each end, wet both ends with warm water, and then overlap the frayed ends in your palm and rub them together until they are felted. The combination of water and friction from the rubbing creates a felted effect.

NOTE: When using hand-dyed yarn, remember to vary skeins throughout garment to maintain color quality.

Vest/Shawl

CO 103 (107, 111, 111) sts. Work patt until piece measures 1½", ending with WS row.

Next row (RS): Work 21 sts in seed st, PM, work 77 (81, 85, 85) sts in St st, PM, work 5 sts in seed st.

Keeping continuity of patt, work until piece measures 18", ending with WS row.

Armhole Row 1 (RS): Keeping continuity of patt, work 21 sts, BO 42 (44, 46, 48) sts, work to end.

Armhole Row 2: Keeping continuity of patt, CO 42 (44, 46, 48) sts over BO sts.

Keeping continuity of patt, work until piece measures 34 (35, 36, 37)".

Work 2nd armhole.

Keeping continuity of patt, work until piece measures 52 (53, 54, 55)".

Finishing

With crochet hook, work 1 rnd sc around armhole openings.

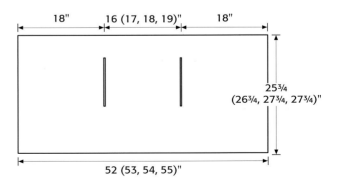

BROKEN GARTER

IN THE KNIT AND PURL CHAPTER, we introduced the idea of color depth. Building on that concept, we would like to illustrate how another combination of knitting and purling can create a different pattern while still enhancing depth of color. The broken garter stitch is a patterned combination of knit and purl stitches, which means that you knit a specific number of stitches and then you purl a specific number of stitches. On subsequent rows, you simply knit the purl stitches and purl the knit stitches.

WITH REGULAR GARTER STITCH, all rows are knit, which forms continuous ridges or stripes in the work. While it's nice for some projects, garter-stitch rows can become monotonous. But broken garter stitch breaks up the monotony and the appearance of rows or stripes.

How does it work? Rather than knitting all stitches on the right-side rows, each pattern will call for some of the stitches to be purled, adding texture to that row. Then on the wrong-side rows, if you see a bump for a completed purl stitch, you will knit, just as in garter stitch. If you see a V for a completed knit stitch in the row below, you will purl. The completed pattern is essentially garter stitch, however, wherever you are directed to purl on right-side rows, you will be breaking up the garter ridge, offsetting it by a row. While broken garter stitch by itself creates an interesting texture, when you work it with two yarns, the garter-ridge rows are blurred and the colors blend quite effectively, enhancing the look of the stitches.

When you read a pattern for broken garter stitch, you will see that the instructions are remarkably simple and deceptively short. There will be instructions for only one row with a note that you repeat that one row throughout the garment. If you follow the pattern without knowing that the trick to broken garter is to knit the opposite of the stitch you see, you may end up creating the stockinette stitch.

There are so many virtues to the broken garter stitch that we're sure you'll like working with it if you haven't already discovered it. It is easy to do, it is a great stitch for combining colors, and it blurs rows to create an impressionist look rather than a strict stripe or ridge effect. And, it lies flat once it is knit. It is wonderful for scarves because it does not curl. You can knit all kinds of garments, including socks, using broken garter stitch.

The four garments in this chapter illustrate how easily the broken garter stitch, when combined with two or more hand-dyed yarns, can make a garment that blends a variety of colors throughout a garment. Four-by-One Short-Sleeved-Sweater, Three-by-Three Vest, Five-by-Two Sweater, and Three-by-Two Socks all illustrate how hand-dyed yarns work effectively with the broken garter stitch.

Four-by-One Short-Sleeved Sweater

SKILL LEVEL: EASY ◖■□▭

FOUR-BY-ONE SHORT-SLEEVED SWEATER is a women's crewneck sweater. This cute sweater is knit with two hand-dyed yarns: one monocolored and one multicolored. The name of this lightweight sweater is derived from the pattern of stitches: knit four, purl one. The stitch pattern gently blends the colors of the lovely pastel yarns. For contrast, the sleeves are knit in stockinette stitch with just one yarn; the multicolored broken garter stitch is used for the edging.

Two different colors of Terrain by Wool in the Woods were used to knit this sweater.

Finished Measurements

Bust: 38 (40½, 43, 46, 48½)"

Length: 21 (22, 23, 24, 24½)"

Materials

A   3 (4, 4, 5, 5) skeins of Wool in the Woods Terrain (80% cotton, 20% rayon; 200 yds/ 183 m per skein), color Azure **4**

B   2 (3, 4, 4, 4) skeins of Wool in the Woods Terrain (80% cotton, 20% rayon; 200 yds/ 183 m per skein), color Spring Garden **4**

•   Size US 7 (4.5 mm) needles or size required to obtain gauge

•   Size US 7 (4.5 mm) 16" circular needles

•   Stitch holders

•   Stitch markers

Gauge

15 sts and 32 rows = 4" in patt

To swatch, CO 16 sts and work patt; measure only 15 sts of swatch.

Four-by-One Pattern

Multiple of 5 + 1 sts

All rows: *P1, K4; rep from * to last st, P1.

Color sequence: Alternate yarns, working 2 rows with A, then 2 rows with B throughout patt.

Stockinette Stitch

All RS rows: Knit.

All WS rows: Purl.

NOTE: When using hand-dyed yarn, remember to vary skeins throughout garment to maintain color quality.

Back

With A, CO 71 (76, 81, 86, 91) sts. Work patt in color sequence until piece measures 13 (13½, 14, 15, 15)".

Armhole shaping: Keeping continuity of patt, BO 3 sts at each side once. BO 2 sts at each side once. Dec 1 st at each side EOR 2 (2, 2, 3, 3) times—57 (62, 67, 70, 75) sts. Work until piece measures 20 (21, 22, 23, 23½)".

Neck shaping: Keeping continuity of patt, work 19 (21, 23, 24, 26) sts, place next 19 (20, 21, 22, 23) sts on holder. Join 2nd ball of yarn and work last 19 (21, 23, 24, 26) sts. Working both sides at same time, BO 2 sts at each neck edge once—17 (19, 21, 22, 24) sts. Work until piece measures 21 (22, 23, 24, 24½)". Place shoulder sts on holder.

Front

Work as for back until piece measures 17½ (18½, 19, 20, 20½)"—57 (62, 67, 70, 75) sts.

Neck shaping: Keeping continuity of patt, work 23 (25, 27, 28, 30) sts, place next 11 (12, 13, 14, 15) sts on holder. Join 2nd ball of yarn and work last 23 (25, 27, 28, 30) sts. Working both sides at same time, BO 2 sts at each neck edge twice. Dec 1 st at each neck edge EOR twice—17 (19, 21, 22, 24) sts. Work until piece measures 21 (22, 23, 24, 24½)". Place shoulder sts on holder.

Sleeves (make 2)

With A, CO 51 (51, 56, 56, 61) sts. Work in patt and color sequence for 8 rows.

With A, work St st, inc 1 st at each side every 4th row once. Inc 1 st at each side EOR 3 (4, 4, 4, 4) times—59 (61, 66, 66, 71) sts. Work even until sleeve measures 3½ (3¾, 3¾, 3¾, 4)".

Cap shaping: Keeping continuity of patt, BO 3 sts at each side once. BO 2 sts at each side once. Dec 1 st at each side EOR 3 (3, 4, 4, 5) times. Dec 1 st at each side every 4th row 9 times—25 (27, 30, 30, 33) sts. BO 3 sts at each side once. BO 2 sts at each side once—15 (17, 20, 20, 23) sts. BO rem sts loosely.

Finishing

Knit shoulder seams tog, using 3-needle BO.

Sew in sleeves.

Sew side seams tog.

Neckband: With RS tog, A, and 16" circular needles, beg at left shoulder seam, PU 13 (14, 13, 15, 14) sts to front holder, K11 (12, 13, 14, 15) sts from holder, PU 12 (14, 13, 14, 13) sts to shoulder seam, PU 5 sts to back holder, K19 (20, 21, 22, 23) sts from holder, and PU 5 sts to shoulder seam; PM and join.

  Rnd 1: Purl.

  Rnd 2: Knit.

  Rnd 3: Purl.

BO loosely in knit.

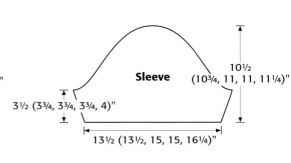

4½ (5, 5½, 5¾, 6½)"

3½"

8 (8½, 9, 9, 9½)"

Back/Front

21 (22, 23, 24, 24½)"

13 (13½, 14, 15, 15)"

19 (20¼, 21½, 23, 24¼)"

3½ (3¾, 3¾, 3¾, 4)"

Sleeve

10½ (10¾, 11, 11, 11¼)"

13½ (13½, 15, 15, 16¼)"

Three-by-Three Vest

SKILL LEVEL: EASY ■■□□

THREE-BY-THREE VEST is a comfortable women's vest made with two multicolored hand-dyed yarns. Though all hand-dyed yarns are unique, the dyeing process for the yarns in this vest was a little different. Most hand-dyed yarn companies must find a way to use up their excess dye. So, they will do a small run of yarn using those excess dyes. At Wool in the Woods, we call colors created this way "Lottery" because the color combinations can be a wonderful surprise—just like winning the lottery. We use different color combinations than we normally would to use up the excess dye, and the resulting yarns will not necessarily ever be repeated.

So, rather than attempting to re-create this vest exactly as pictured, simply choose two multi-colored hand-dyed yarns and create your own one-of-a-kind vest. By using the broken garter stitch in a knit three—purl three repeat, all the colors will blend throughout the garment. Then, to let each yarn shine on its own, we used one of the yarns alone to do a garter-stitch armhole edging, and the other yarn to do the same around the neck edge.

The Three-by-Three Vest was knit using Bobcat by Wool in the Woods in two different lottery color variations.

Finished Measurements

Bust: 40 (42¾, 46¼, 49½)"

Length: 21½ (22½, 23½, 24½)"

Materials

A   2 (3, 3, 4) skeins of Wool in the Woods Bobcat (100% wool; 200 yds/183 m per skein), color Lottery (5)

B   2 (3, 3, 4) skeins of Wool in the Woods Bobcat (100% wool; 200 yds/183 m per skein), color Lottery (5)

• Size US 10½ (6.5 mm) needles or size required to obtain gauge

• 7 buttons, ⅞" diameter

• Stitch holders

• Stitch markers

Gauge

14 sts and 28 rows = 4" in patt

To swatch, CO 15 sts and work patt; measure only 14 sts of swatch.

Three-by-Three Pattern

Multiple of 6 + 3 sts

All rows: *K3, P3; rep from * to last 3 sts, K3.

Color sequence: Alternate yarns, working 2 rows with A, then 2 rows with B throughout.

NOTE: When using hand-dyed yarn, remember to vary skeins throughout garment to maintain color quality.

Back

With A, CO 69 (75, 81, 87) sts. Work patt in color sequence until piece measures 12 (13, 13½, 14½)".

Armhole shaping: Keeping continuity of patt, BO 3 sts at each side once. BO 2 sts at each side once. Dec 1 st at each side EOR 4 times—51 (57, 63, 69) sts. Work until piece measures 20½ (21½, 22½, 23½)".

Neck shaping: Keeping continuity of patt, work 16 (18, 20, 22) sts, place next 19 (21, 23, 25) sts on holder. Join 2nd ball of yarn and work last 16 (18, 20, 22) sts. Working both sides at same time, BO 2 sts at each neck edge once—14 (16, 18, 20) sts.

Work until piece measures 21½ (22½, 23½, 24½)". Place shoulder sts on holder.

Fronts (work both pieces at same time)

CO 35 (38, 41, 44) sts for each front. Work patt in color sequence as foll until pieces measure 12 (13, 13½, 14¼)".

LEFT FRONT

Row 1 (RS): *K3, P3; rep from * to last 5 (2, 5, 2) sts, K3 (2, 3, 2), P2 (0, 2, 0).

Row 2: P2 (0, 2, 0), K3 (2, 3, 2) *K3, P3; rep from * to end.

RIGHT FRONT

Row 1 (RS): K0 (2, 0, 2), P2 (3, 2, 3) *K3, P3; rep from * to last 3 sts, K3.

Row 2: *K3, P3; rep from * to last 5 (2, 5, 2) sts, K3 (2, 3, 2), P2 (0, 2, 0).

SHAPING

Armhole shaping: Keeping continuity of patt, foll armhole shaping as for back—26 (29, 32, 35) sts. Work until pieces measure 18½ (19½, 20½, 21)".

Neck shaping: Keeping continuity of patt, BO 4 sts at each neck edge once. BO 3 sts at each neck edge 1 (1, 1, 2) time(s). BO 2 sts at each neck edge 1 (2, 2, 1) time(s). Dec 1 st EOR 3 (2, 3, 3) times—14 (16, 18, 20) sts. Work until pieces measure 21½ (22½, 23½, 24½)". Place shoulder sts on holder.

Finishing

Knit shoulder seams tog, using 3-needle BO.

Armhole bands: With A, PU and knit 1 st in each garter-st ridge, adjusting as necessary through bind offs; PM and join. Knit 3 rows. BO loosely in knit.

Sew side seams tog.

Neckband: With RS tog and A, beg at right neck edge, PU 18 (18, 18, 19) sts to shoulder seam, PU 5 sts to back holder, PU 19 (21, 23, 25) sts from holder, PU 5 sts to shoulder seam, and PU 18 (18, 18, 19) sts to left front edge. Knit 3 rows. BO loosely in knit.

Right front band: Measure right front 1" from neck edge, PM. Measure 15" from neck edge, PM. Place 5 more buttonhole markers evenly spaced between 2 markers just placed. With B, PU 1 st in each garter-st ridge and work as foll:

> **Row 1 (WS):** Knit, BO 2 sts at each buttonhole marker.
>
> **Row 2:** Knit, CO 2 sts over BO sts.
>
> **Row 3:** Knit.
>
> BO loosely in knit.

Left front band: Work as for right front band, eliminating buttonholes.

Sew buttons to left front band.

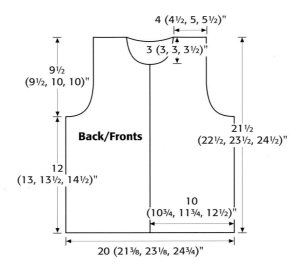

Five-by-Two Sweater

SKILL LEVEL: EASY ■■□□

FIVE-BY-TWO SWEATER is a women's high—V-neck sweater. This lush sweater is knit with three different multicolored hand-dyed yarns. We used richly colored yarns, and to blend them gently, we used a pattern of five knit stitches and two purl stitches throughout the garment. By knitting with each yarn one row at a time, the colors blend throughout the garment, and the mohair softly blurs any appearance of lines. To finish the sweater, the neckband was worked in regular garter stitch.

The Five-by-Two Sweater was knit using the hand-dyed yarns Cyclone, Miss Mohair, and Brown Bear, all by Wool in the Woods.

Finished Measurements

Bust: 38½ (41½, 45, 48½, 51½)"

Length: 21½ (22½, 23½, 24½, 25½)"

Materials

A 3 (3, 4, 4, 4) skeins of Wool in the Woods Cyclone (100% wool; 200 yds/183 m per skein), color Soft Spritz 【4】

B 3 (3, 4, 4, 4) skeins of Wool in the Woods Miss Mohair (78% mohair, 13% wool, 9% nylon; 200 yds/183 m per skein), color Lapis Limits 【4】

C 3 (3, 4, 4, 4) skeins of Wool in the Woods Brown Bear (75% cotton, 12% linen, 10% rayon, 3% nylon; 200 yds/183 m per skein), color Lottery 【3】

- Size US 7 (4.5 mm) needles or size required to obtain gauge
- Size US 6 (4 mm) 16" circular needles
- Stitch holders
- Stitch markers (split-ring variety)

Gauge

17 sts and 32 rows = 4" in pattern on larger needles

To swatch, CO 19 sts and work patt. Measure only 17 sts of swatch.

Five-by-Two Pattern

Multiple of 7 + 5 sts

All rows: *K5, P2; rep from * to last 5 sts, K5.

Color sequence:
> **Row 1:** A
>
> **Row 2:** B
>
> **Row 3:** C

Work these 3 rows consecutively in patt.

NOTE: When using hand-dyed yarn, remember to vary skeins throughout garment to maintain color quality.

Back

With A and larger needles, CO 82 (89, 96, 103, 110) sts. Work patt in color sequence until piece measures 12 (12½, 13½, 14½, 15)".

Armhole shaping: Keeping continuity of patt, BO 2 sts at each side once. Dec 1 st at each side EOR 3 (2, 3, 2, 3) times—72 (81, 86, 95, 100) sts. Work until piece measures 20½ (21½, 22½, 23½, 24½)".

Neck shaping: Keeping continuity of patt, work 24 (28, 30, 33, 34) sts, place next 24 (25, 26, 29, 32) sts on a holder. Join 2nd ball of yarn and work last 24 (28, 30, 33, 34) sts. Working both sides at same time, BO 2 sts at each neck edge once—22 (26, 28, 31, 32) sts.

Work until piece measures 21½ (22½, 23½, 24½, 25½)". Place shoulder sts on holder.

Front

Work as for back until piece measures 15½ (16½, 17½, 18, 19)".

Neck shaping: Keeping continuity of patt, work 36 (40, 43, 47, 50) sts, place next 0 (1, 0, 1, 0) sts on a split-ring marker to act as a st holder. Join 2nd ball of yarn and work last 36 (40, 43, 47, 50) sts. Working both sides at same time, dec 1 st at each neck edge EOR 6 (6, 7, 8, 10) times. Dec 1 st at each neck edge every 4th row 8 times—22 (26, 28, 31, 32) sts.

Keeping continuity of patt, work until piece measures 21½ (22½, 23½, 24½, 25½)". Place shoulder sts on holder.

Sleeves (make 2)

With A and larger needles, CO 33 (40, 40, 40, 47) sts. Work 4 rows even in patt. Keeping continuity of patt, inc 1 st at each side every 6th row 3 (2, 2, 2, 2) times. Inc 1 st at each side every 4th row 13 (12,

12, 12, 11) times. Inc 1 st at each side every 8th row 8 times—81 (84, 84, 84, 89) sts. Work even until sleeve measures 15½ (16, 16½, 17, 17½)".

Cap shaping: Keeping continuity of patt, BO 2 sts at each side once, dec 1 st at each side EOR 3 (2, 3, 2, 3) times, BO 6 sts at each side 3 times—35 (40, 38, 40, 43) sts. BO rem sts loosely.

Finishing

Knit shoulder seams tog, using 3-needle BO.

Sew in sleeves.

Sew side seams tog.

Neckband: With RS tog and smaller, 16" circular needles, beg at left shoulder seam, PU 37 (38, 39, 42, 43) sts to marked st or center of V, knit marked 0 (1, 0, 1, 0) st, PU 37 (38, 39, 42, 43) sts to shoulder seam, PU 6 sts to back holder, K24 (25, 26, 29, 32) sts from holder, PU 6 sts to shoulder seam, PM. Purl 1 rnd. For sizes 38½", 45", and 51½", K35 (37, 41), K2tog tbl, K2tog, knit to end of rnd. For sizes 41½" and 48½", knit to 1 st before marked st, ssk, knit to end of rnd. BO in purl.

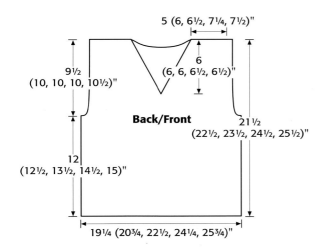

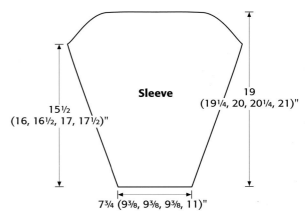

Three-by-Two Socks

SKILL LEVEL: INTERMEDIATE ◖■■▢

 **THREE-BY-TWO SOCKS** are accessories for adult women. We have found that when knitters think of using broken garter, they rarely consider making socks. So, we designed these socks for a monocolored and a multicolored hand-dyed yarn with broken garter stitch in mind. By knitting with each yarn for two rows at a time, the socks are more colorful. The name of these socks comes from the stitch pattern. In this case, you will knit three stitches and then purl two stitches in the broken garter portion of the socks. Then on the next round, you will purl three and knit two. Please don't forget: with socks, you are working in the round and therefore always working from the right side.

To ensure that the socks are comfortable as well as fashionable, the knitting around the foot is done in stockinette stitch so that the fabric is smooth. The broken garter stitch is used on the cuff or leg portion to make the socks colorful, fashionable, and downright fun. This sock pattern offers another unusual yet incredibly simple feature: the top of the socks is knit by using an invisible cast on, which allows you to go back and pick up live stitches to work a tubular bind off.

Two different colors of Twin Twist by Wool in the Woods were used to knit these socks.

Size

One size fits most adult women.

Materials

A 1 skein of Wool in the Woods Twin Twist (92% wool, 8% nylon; 200 yds/183 m per skein), color Raspberry Fizz 🧶③

B 1 skein of Wool in the Woods Twin Twist (92% wool, 8% nylon; 200 yds/183 m per skein), color Just For Fun 🧶③

• Small amount of waste yarn

• 2 pairs of size US 3 (3.25 mm) 24" circular needles or size required to obtain gauge

• Size F (3.75 mm) crochet hook

• Stitch markers

Gauge

26 sts and 36 rows = 4" in St st

Three-by-Two Pattern

Multiple of 5 sts

Rnd 1: With B, *K3, P2; rep from * around.

Rnd 2: With B, *P3, K2; rep from * around.

Rnd 3: With A, *K3, P2; rep from * around.

Rnd 4: With A, *P3, K2; rep from * around.

These 4 rnds form patt.

Leg

With waste yarn and crochet hook, chain 50. (See "Chain Stitch" on page 17.) Using A and 1 pair of circular needles, PU 1 st in each loop of the crocheted chain—50 sts. Divide sts onto 2 circular needles, with 25 sts on each needle, and join.

Work K1, P1 ribbing until sock measures ¾". Knit 1 row.

Work in patt, alternating A and B yarns until sock measures 3¾".

Dec rnd: With A, knit rnd, dec 5 sts evenly around—45 sts. Cont in St st with A until sock measures 4½".

Work patt until sock measures 6".

Dec rnd: With A, knit rnd, dec 1 st—44 sts. Make sure there are 22 sts on each needle.

Knit 2 rnds. Do not cut A.

Heel Flap

With B, work reinforced heel back and forth on 22 sts and 1 pair of circular needles, as foll:

> **Row 1:** Sl 1 pw, *K1, sl 1 pw; rep from * to last st, K1.
>
> **Row 2:** Sl 1 pw, purl to end.

Work this 2-row rep 11 times.

Heel Turning

Cont with B and work the foll 9 rows:

> **Row 1:** K12, K2tog, K1, turn.
>
> **Row 2:** Sl 1, P5, ssp, P1, turn.
>
> **Row 3:** Sl 1, K6, K2tog, K1, turn.
>
> **Row 4:** Sl 1, P7, ssp, P1, turn.
>
> **Row 5:** Sl 1, K8, K2tog, K1, turn.
>
> **Row 6:** Sl 1, P9, ssp, P1, turn.
>
> **Row 7:** Sl 1, K10, K2tog, K1, turn.
>
> **Row 8:** Sl 1, P11, ssp, turn.
>
> **Row 9:** K14; cut B.

Gusset

With A that is attached to leg, PU 1 st in space between instep sts and heel flap, PU 11 sts along right side of heel flap. Knit across 7 sts of heel. With other pair of needles, knit rem 7 sts of heel. PU 11 sts along left side of heel flap, PU 1 st in space between heel flap and instep sts. Knit 11 sts of instep to this needle—30 sts on each pair of circular needles. We have just made a 90° turn in the sock and will continue this orientation throughout.

Rnd 1: K11, K2tog, PM, knit to end of first needle. Knit to last 13 sts, PM, ssk, knit to end of second needle.

Rnd 2: Knit.

Work these 2 rnds until 22 sts rem on each needle.

Foot

Knit all rnds even (22 sts per needle) until sock measures 2" shorter than desired length.

Toe

Change to B and work foll rnds:

> **Rnd 1:** Knit.
>
> **Rnd 2:** [K8, ssk, K2, K2tog, K8] twice.
>
> **Rnds 3 and 4:** Knit.
>
> **Rnd 5:** [K7, ssk, K2, K2tog, K7] twice.
>
> **Rnds 6 and 7:** Knit.
>
> **Rnd 8:** [K6, ssk, K2, K2tog, K6] twice.
>
> **Rnd 9:** Knit.

Work rest of toe as rnds 8 and 9, knitting 1 less st before and after dec until 4 sts rem on each needle. Knit 2 sts from first needle to second needle. Knit 2 sts from second needle and knit 2 sts from first needle. We have just made a 90° turn in the sock. Weave 4 sts on first needle with 4 sts from second needle, referring to "Kitchener Stitch" on page 18.

Tubular Bind Off

Pull out crochet chain at top of sock, PU 1 st from each chain st as you go along. Place 25 sts on each pair of circular needles.

Inc rnd: [*K1, inc 1 st in next st; rep from * to last 3 sts, K3] twice—36 sts each pair of needles.

Rnd 1: *K1, sl 1 wyif; rep from * around.

Rnd 2: *Sl 1 wyib, P1; rep from * around.

Work this 2-rnd rep a total of 3 times.

Pull out first needle. Half of sts will fall to back, and half will fall forward. Place back 18 sts on spare needle or holder and place front 18 sts on needle. Work Kitchener st to join.

Rep for sts on second needle.

TRIMS AND ACCENTS

DO YOU WANT TO ADD SOME COLOR TO A GARMENT? Would you like to enhance a sweater, vest, or scarf by adding a different texture? Adding some edging, a little trim, a delicate neckline, colorful cuffs, multiple joinings, or a few stripes is simple to do yet offers countless rewards. With the seemingly never-ending selection of hand-dyed yarns available today, you can "dress up" a basic garment with ease.

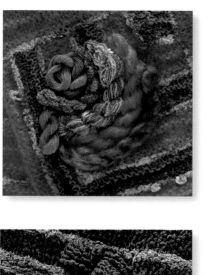

L ET'S SAY THAT YOU ARE MAKING a mono-colored sweater, but you would like to be able to wear it with many different items in your wardrobe. By adding a multicolored edge or a couple of stripes, you will increase your wardrobe possibilities and still keep the emphasis on the original color. So many of us find ourselves attracted to a yarn that we think is too exotic to use for an entire garment. By knitting a trim or accent with this yarn, you will be able to use it without feeling overwhelmed by its flair. If you like clothing that is simple and elegant without too many colors or designs, but you do not want to have all of your clothing be monochromatic, add a multi-colored trim.

It is also easy to add color throughout a garment. One way is knitting in blocks. If you would like to add some color to a garment with blocks, why not use a multicolored hand-dyed yarn? Your garment will be more colorful and the texture of the entire garment will be enriched.

The hand-dyed yarns that are available today provide everything from natural fibers to metallic fibers to real or faux fur. Just imagine all of the possibilities for your wardrobe!

The four garments in this chapter illustrate how a simple trim or accent can change the look of a garment. Textured Miter, Nights in Natchez, Tough to Beat, and All Turned Around illustrate just a few of the countless ways that you can use hand-dyed yarn to add a little color or texture to a garment.

Textured Miter

 **TEXTURED MITER** is a women's scarf in which the shape, design, and hand-dyed yarns meld to create a stunning accessory. The scarf is made with four monocolored hand-dyed yarns and one multicolored hand-dyed yarn, which is used to accent the other yarns. All five yarns are used in knitting the striped, mitered square of the scarf, while only two, the blue mohair and the multicolored accent yarn, are used to knit the remainder of the project. Though this scarf looks complex, it uses only stockinette and garter stitch. This is a wonderful example of how you can use items from your stash to accent a garment.

The following yarns unite to produce this lovely scarf: Tribbles by Great Adirondack Yarn Company and Miss Mohair, Feel'n Fuzzy, Wilkson, and Southern Rose by Wool in the Woods.

Finished Measurements

Length: 47" each side

Materials

A 2 skeins of Wool in the Woods Miss Mohair (78% mohair, 13% wool, 9% nylon; 200 yds/183 m per skein), color Bluebird **4**

B 2 skeins of Great Adirondack Tribbles (80% rayon, 20% cotton; 60 yds/55 m per skein), color Hydrangea **5**

C 1 skein Wool in the Woods Feel'n Fuzzy (90% kid mohair, 10% nylon; 200 yds/183 m per skein), color Groovy Grape **1**

D 1 skein Wool in the Woods Wilkson (93% wool, 7% nylon; 200 yds/183 m per skein), color Red Red Wine **2**

E 1 skein Wool in the Woods Southern Rose (55% mohair, 45% merino wool; 200 yds/183 m per skein), color More Than Mint **4**

• Size US 11 (8 mm) needles or size required to obtain gauge

Gauge

11 sts and 14 rows = 4" in St st with A

Stripe Pattern

Rows 1–3, 5–7, and 9–11: With A, knit.

Rows 4, 8, and 12: With A, purl.

Rows 13 and 14: With B, knit.

These 14 rows form patt.

NOTE: When using hand-dyed yarn, remember to vary skeins throughout garment to maintain color quality.

Mitered Square

With A, use a long-tail CO (see page 16) to loosely CO 61 sts. This is row 1.

Row 2 (WS): With A, K1tbl, K28, K3tog, K28, sl 1 wyif.

Row 3: K1tbl, knit to last st, sl 1 wyif.

Row 18: K1tbl, K20, K3tog, K20, sl 1 wyif.

Row 19: K1tbl, knit to last st, sl 1 wyif.

Row 20: K1tbl, P19, P3tog, P19, sl 1.

Row 21: K1tbl, knit to last st, sl 1 wyif.

Row 22: K1tbl, K18, K3tog, K18, sl 1 wyif.

Row 23: K1tbl, knit to last st, sl 1 wyif.

Row 24: K1tbl, P17, P3tog, P17, sl 1.

Row 25: Change to B, K1tbl, knit to last st, sl 1 wyif.

Row 26: K1tbl, K16, K3tog, K16, sl 1 wyif.

Row 27: Change to C and D held tog, K1tbl, knit to last st, sl 1 wyif.

Row 28: K1tbl, K15, K3tog, K15, sl 1 wyif.

Row 29: K1tbl, knit to last st, sl 1 wyif.

Row 30: K1tbl, P14, P3tog, P14, sl 1 wyif.

Row 31: Change to E, K1tbl, knit to last st, sl 1 wyif.

Row 32: K1tbl, K13, K3tog, K13, sl 1 wyif.

Row 4: K1tbl, P27, P3tog, P27, sl 1.

Row 5: Change to B, K1tbl, knit to last st, sl 1 wyif.

Row 6: K1tbl, K26, K3tog, K26, sl 1 wyif.

Row 7: Change to C and D held tog, K1tbl, knit to last st, sl 1 wyif.

Row 8: K1tbl, K25, K3tog, K25, sl 1 wyif.

Row 9: K1tbl, knit to last st, sl 1 wyif.

Row 10: K1tbl, P24, P3tog, P24, sl 1 wyif.

Row 11: Change to E, K1tbl, knit to last st, sl 1 wyif,.

Row 12: K1tbl, K23, K3tog, K23, sl 1 wyif.

Row 13: K1tbl, knit to last st, sl 1 wyif.

Row 14: K1tbl, P22, P3tog, P22, sl 1 wyif.

Row 15: Change to B, K1tbl, knit to last st, sl 1 wyif.

Row 16: K1tbl, K21, K3tog, K21, sl 1 wyif.

Row 17: Change to A, K1tbl, knit to last st, sl 1 wyif.

Row 33: K1tbl, knit to last st, sl 1 wyif.

Row 34: K1tbl, P12, P3tog, P12, sl 1 wyif.

Row 35: Change to B, K1tbl, knit to last st, sl 1 wyif.

Row 36: K1tbl, K11, K3tog, K11, sl 1 wyif.

Row 37: Change to A, K1tbl, knit to last st, sl 1 wyif.

Row 38: K1tbl, K10, K3tog, K10, sl 1 wyif.

Row 39: K1tbl, knit to last st, sl 1 wyif.

Row 40: K1tbl, P9, P3tog, P9, sl 1 wyif.

Row 41: K1tbl, knit to last st, sl 1 wyif.

Row 42: K1tbl, K8, K3tog, K8, sl 1 wyif.

Row 43: K1tbl, knit to last st, sl 1 wyif.

Row 44: K1tbl, P7, P3tog, P7, sl 1 wyif.

Row 45: Change to B, K1tbl, knit to last st, sl 1 wyif.

Row 46: K1tbl, K6, K3tog, K6, sl 1 wyif.

Row 47: Change to C and D held tog, K5tbl, knit to last st, sl 1 wyif.

Row 48: K1tbl, K5, K3tog, K5, sl 1 wyif.

Row 49: K1tbl, knit to last st, sl 1 wyif.

Row 50: K1tbl, P4, P3tog, P4, sl 1 wyif.

Row 51: Change to E, K1tbl, knit to last st, sl 1 wyif.

Row 52: K1tbl, K3, K3tog, K3, sl 1 wyif.

Row 53: K1tbl, knit to last st, sl 1 wyif.

Row 54: K1tbl, P2, P3tog, P2, sl 1 wyif.

Row 55: Change to B, K1tbl, knit to last st, sl 1 wyif.

Row 56: K1tbl, K1, K3tog, K1, sl 1 wyif.

Row 57: K1tbl, knit to last st, sl 1 wyif.

Row 58: K1tbl, K3tog, sl 1 wyif.

Row 59: K3tog.

Scarf Sides

With B and RS tog, PU 30 sts along a multicolored side of mitered square.

With B, knit 1 row. Work stripe patt until piece measures 47", ending with row 14. BO loosely in knit.

PU 30 sts along other striped edge of mitered square and work stripe patt as described above.

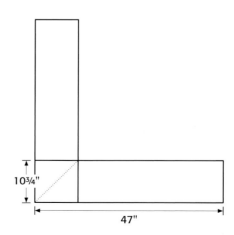

10¾"

47"

Nights in Natchez

SKILL LEVEL: INTERMEDIATE ◼◼◼▭

 **NIGHTS IN NATCHEZ** is a women's cardigan made with one monocolored and one multicolored hand-dyed yarn. The body of the cardigan is knit in shaker rib stitch. The accent trim around the wristbands and the two stripes on the bottom of the cardigan are knit in stockinette stitch. The sweater clearly shows the color variation in the monocolored yarn. The multicolored accents draw those variations together while also adding some other colors to the garment. The freshwater-pearl buttons on this sweater have variations in color that are a wonderful complement to the hand-dyed yarns. The yarns Cleo by Prism Arts, Inc. and Reflections by Wool in the Woods merge to make this impressive cardigan.

Finished Measurements

Bust: 37½ (40, 42¼, 44½, 46¾)"

Length: 20½ (21, 22, 23, 23½)"

Materials

A   2 (2, 3, 3, 4) skeins of Prism Cleo (90% rayon, 10% polyester; 82 yds/75 m, 1.5 oz per skein), color Alpine ⬤4

B   6 (6, 7, 7, 8) skeins of Wool in the Woods Reflections (80% cotton, 20% rayon; 200 yds/183 m per skein), color Heather ⬤3

•   Size US 6 (4 mm) needles or size required to obtain gauge

•   8 buttons, ¾" diameter

•   Stitch holders

•   Stitch markers

Gauge

21 sts and 38 rows = 4" in patt

Shaker Rib Pattern

Row 1 (RS): P1, *K1 in st below, P1; rep from * to end.

Row 2: Knit.

These 2 rows form patt.

Stockinette Stitch

All RS rows: Knit.

All WS rows: Purl.

NOTE: When using hand-dyed yarn, remember to vary skeins throughout garment to maintain color quality.

Back

With A, CO 75 (79, 83, 87, 91) sts. Work 8 rows St st, ending with WS row.

With B, knit 1 row, inc 24 (26, 28, 30, 32) sts evenly spaced across row—99 (105, 111, 117, 123) sts. Knit next row.

Work rib patt row for 9 rows, ending with row 1.

Next row (WS): K1, *P1, K1; rep from * to end.

With A (RS), knit 1 row, dec 24 (26, 28, 30, 32) sts evenly spaced across row—75 (79, 83, 87, 91) sts. Work St st for a total of 6 rows.

With B (RS), knit 1 row, inc 24 (26, 28, 30, 32) sts evenly spaced across row—99 (105, 111, 117, 123) sts. Knit next row. Work in patt until piece measures 11½ (12, 13, 13, 13½)".

Armhole shaping: Keeping continuity of patt, BO 4 sts at each armhole edge once. BO 3 sts at each armhole edge once. BO 2 sts at each armhole edge once. Dec as foll:

> Row I (RS): K3, K2tog tbl, work patt to last 5 sts, K2tog, K3.
>
> Row 2 (WS): P3, work patt to last 3 sts, P3.

Work dec rows 6 times—69 (75, 81, 87, 93) sts.

Work in patt until piece measures 19½ (20, 21, 22, 22½)".

> The underarm finishing will be neater if you K1, P1 on wrong-side rows through the bind offs, then knit the rest of each row.

Neck shaping: Keeping continuity of patt, work 22 (24, 26, 28, 30) sts, place next 25 (27, 29, 31, 33) sts on holder. Join 2nd ball of yarn and work last 22 (24, 26, 28, 30) sts. Working both sides at same time, BO 2 sts at each neck edge once—20 (22, 24, 26, 28) sts. Work until piece measures 20½ (21, 22, 23, 23½)". Place shoulder sts on holder.

Fronts (work both pieces at same time)

With A, CO 37 (39, 41, 43, 45) sts for each front. Work 8 rows St st, ending with WS row.

With B, knit 1 row, inc 12 (14, 14, 16, 16) sts evenly spaced across row—49 (53, 55, 59, 61) sts. Knit next row. Work rib patt for 9 rows, ending with row 1.

Next row (WS): K1, *P1, K1; rep from * to end.

With A, knit 1 row, dec 12 (14, 14, 16, 16) sts evenly spaced across row—37 (39, 41, 43, 45) sts. Work St st for a total of 6 rows.

With B (RS), knit 1 row, inc 12 (14, 14, 16, 16) sts evenly spaced across row—49 (53, 55, 59, 61) sts. Knit next row. Work patt until piece measures 11½ (12, 13, 13, 13½)".

Armhole shaping: Keeping continuity of patt, work armhole dec as for back—34 (38, 40, 44, 46) sts. Work until pieces measure 17½ (18, 19, 20, 20½)".

Neck shaping: Keeping continuity of patt, BO 5 sts at each neck edge once. BO 4 sts at each neck edge once. BO 3 sts at each neck edge once. BO 2 sts at each neck edge 0 (1, 1, 2, 2) time(s). Dec 1 st EOR twice—20 (22, 24, 26, 28) sts. Work until pieces measure 20½ (21, 22, 23, 23½)". Place shoulder sts on holder.

Sleeves (make 2)

With A, CO 29 (29, 33, 33, 37) sts. Work 8 rows St st, ending with WS row.

With B, knit 1 row, inc 8 sts evenly spaced across row—37 (37, 41, 41, 45) sts. Knit next row.

Work rib patt for 9 rows, inc 1 st at each side every 4th row twice—41 (41, 45, 45, 49) sts—and ending with row 1.

Next row (WS): K1, *P1, K1; rep from * to end.

With A, knit 1 row, dec 8 sts evenly spaced across row—33 (33, 37, 37, 41) sts. Work in St st for a total of 6 rows.

With B, knit 1 row, inc 8 sts evenly spaced across row—41 (41, 45, 45, 49) sts. Knit next row.

Work in patt for 9 rows, inc 1 st at each side every 4th row twice—45 (45, 49, 49, 53) sts—and ending with row 1.

Next row (WS): K1, *P1, K1; rep from * to end.

With A, knit 1 row, dec 8 sts evenly spaced across row—37 (37, 41, 41, 45) sts. Work in St st for a total of 4 rows.

With B, knit 1 row, inc 8 sts evenly spaced across row—45 (45, 49, 49, 53) sts. Knit next row.

Keeping continuity of patt, inc 1 st at each side every 4th row 11 times—67 (67, 71, 71, 75) sts. Inc 1 st at each side every 6th row 3 times—73 (73, 77, 77, 81) sts. Work in patt until sleeve measures 15 (15½, 16, 16½, 17)".

Cap shaping: Keeping continuity of patt, BO 4 sts at each side once. BO 3 sts at each side once. BO 2 sts at each side once—55 (55, 59, 59, 63) sts. Dec as foll:

> **Row 1:** K3, K2tog tbl, work patt to last 5 sts, K2tog, K3.

> **Row 2:** P3, work patt to last 3 sts, P3.

Work dec rows 16 times—23 (23, 27, 27, 31) sts. BO rem sts loosely.

Finishing

Knit shoulder seams tog, using 3-needle BO.

Sew in sleeves.

Sew side seams tog.

Neckband: With RS tog and B, beg at right neck edge, PU 19 (19, 20, 20, 21) sts to shoulder seam, PU 4 sts to holder, K25 (27, 29, 31, 33) sts from holder, PU 4 sts to shoulder seam, PU 19 (19, 20, 20, 21) sts to left front edge. Work in garter st for 5 rows. BO loosely in knit.

Right front band: On right front, measure 1" down from neck edge and PM; measure 1" up from bottom edge and PM. Place 6 more button-hole markers evenly spaced between 2 markers just placed. With B, PU 88 (90, 93, 96, 97) sts along right front and work as foll:

> **Row 1 (WS):** Knit, BO 2 sts at each marker.

> **Row 2:** Knit, CO 2 sts over each BO st.

> **Rows 3–5:** Knit.

BO loosely in knit.

Left front band: With B, PU (88, 90, 93, 96, 98) sts along left front. Knit 5 rows. BO loosely in knit. Sew buttons to left front band.

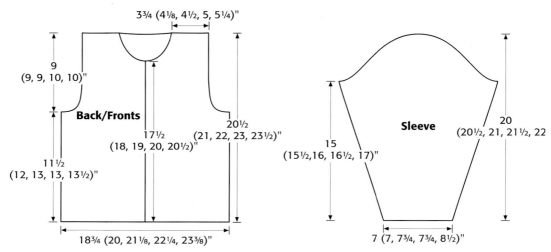

Tough to Beat

SKILL LEVEL: EASY ■■□□

 TOUGH TO BEAT is a women's vest made with one monocolored and one multicolored hand-dyed yarn. This casual vest is knit all in one piece, and the shoulders are knit together, so no sewing is involved! The body is knit in stockinette stitch, while the accent stripes and edging are worked in garter stitch. This fashionable vest is particularly intriguing because of its stripes. So many people shy away from wearing stripes because they tend to make a person look wider. As the fashion experts have found, if you break up the uniformity of the stripes, your eye no longer looks side to side, but up and down. So everyone can enjoy wearing stripes!

Two yarns were combined to create this vest: Pizazz and Shaggy, both by Wool in the Woods.

Finished Measurements

Bust: 37¼ (39¼, 41¼, 43¼, 45¼)"

Length: 20 (20, 21, 22, 23)"

Materials

A   2 (2, 3, 3, 4) skeins of Wool in the Woods Pizazz (100% wool; 200 yds/183 m per skein), color Groovy Grape (5)

B   2 (2, 3, 3, 4) skeins of Wool in the Woods Shaggy (75% rayon, 25% polyester; 200 yds/ 183 m per skein), color Juniper (3)

•   Size US 10½ (6.5 mm) straight and 24" circular needles or size required to obtain gauge

•   Size US 10½ (6.5 mm) 16" circular needles

•   5 buttons, ⅞" diameter

•   Stitch holders

•   Stitch markers

Gauge

12 sts and 14 rows = 4" in patt

Stripe Pattern

Rows 1–4: With A, work in St st.

Rows 5 and 6: With 2 strands of B held tog, work in garter st.

Rows 7–16: With A, work in St st.

Rows 17 and 18: With 2 strands of B held tog, work in garter st.

Rows 19–24: With A, work in St st.

Rows 25–28: With 2 strands of B held tog, work in garter st.

These 28 rows form patt.

NOTE: When using hand-dyed yarn, remember to vary skeins throughout garment to maintain color quality.

Body

With larger needles and 2 strands of B held tog, CO 112 (118, 124, 130, 136) sts. Knit 1 row (WS).

Change to 1 strand of A and begin stripe patt. Work in patt until piece measures 11½ (11, 12, 12, 13)".

Split for fronts and back: Work 26 (28, 29, 31, 32) sts, BO 4 sts, work 52 (54, 58, 60, 64) sts, BO 4 sts, work 26 (28, 29, 31, 32) sts. Sl first 26 (28, 29, 31, 32) sts to needle with last 26 (28, 29, 31, 32) sts for fronts. Place back 52 (54, 58, 60, 64) sts on holder.

Fronts (work both pieces at same time)

Armhole and neck shaping: Keeping continuity of patt, BO 2 sts at each armhole edge once. Dec 1 st at each armhole edge EOR 3 times. AT SAME TIME, when pieces measure 12 (12, 13, 13½, 14½)", dec 1 st at each neck edge EOR 8 times. Dec 1 st at each neck edge every 4th row 5 times—8 (10, 11, 13,

14) sts. Work until pieces measure 20 (20, 21, 22, 23)". Place shoulder sts on holder.

Back

Sl 52 (54, 58, 60, 64) sts from holder to needle. Keeping continuity of patt, work armhole dec as for fronts—42 (44, 48, 50, 54) sts. Work until piece measures 19 (19, 20, 21, 22)".

Neck shaping: Keeping continuity of patt, work 10 (12, 13, 15, 16) sts, place next 22 (20, 22, 20, 22) sts on holder. Join 2nd ball of yarn and work last 10 (12, 13, 15, 16) sts. Working both sides at same time, BO 2 sts at each neck edge once—8 (10, 11, 13, 14) sts. Work until piece measures 20 (20, 21, 22, 23)". Place shoulder sts on holder.

Finishing

Knit shoulder seams tog, using 3-needle BO.

Armhole bands: With RS tog, B, and 16" circular needles, PU 64 (66, 66, 68, 68) sts around armhole edge.

> **Rnd 1:** Purl.
>
> **Rnd 2:** Knit.
>
> BO loosely in purl.

Front and neckbands: On right front, place 5 markers evenly spaced from V-neck to bottom for buttonholes. With B and RS tog, use 24" circular needles and PU 38 (38, 40, 41, 43) sts from right bottom front to V-neck, PU 33 sts to shoulder seam, PU 3 sts to back holder, K22 (20, 22, 20, 22) sts from back holder, PU 3 sts to shoulder seam, PU 33 sts to front V-neck, and 38 (38, 40, 41, 43) sts to bottom left front.

> **Row 1:** Knit, BO 1 st at each marker for buttonhole.
>
> **Row 2:** Knit, CO 1 st over BO sts.
>
> **Row 3:** Knit.
>
> BO loosely in knit.

Sew buttons to left front band.

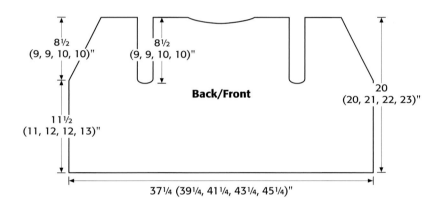

All Turned Around

 **ALL TURNED AROUND** is a delicate women's tank top made with one monocolored and one multicolored hand-dyed yarn. In this garment we attempted to make the most of all of the colors. As you can see in the photograph, the body of the tank top is lime green. Interestingly enough, the accent yarn does not contain any lime green. Because the yarns do not share the same colors, the accent colors really stand out. The body of the tank top is knit in stockinette stitch while the edging and stripes are knit with an eyelet stitch. The tank is knit in side-to-side panels for the bottom, and the stitches are picked up along one selvage edge to complete the yokes.

Two yarns combine to make this lovely tank top: Cha Cha by Great Adirondack Yarn Company and Cruz by Wool in the Woods.

Finished Measurements

Bust: 36 (38, 41, 44)"

Length: 21 (22, 22, 23)"

Materials

A   3 (4, 4, 5) skeins of Wool in the Woods Cruz (100% rayon; 200 yds/183 m per skein), color Limelight (3)

B   2 (3, 4, 5) skeins of Great Adirondack Cha Cha (90% cotton 10% polyester; 100 yds/92 m per skein), color Grenada (3)

- Size US 5 (3.75 mm) 16" and 24" circular needles or size required to obtain gauge

- Stitch holders

- Stitch markers

Gauge

24 sts and 30 rows = 4" in patt

Eyelet Pattern

Row 1 (RS): With B, K2, *yo, K3, then with left-hand needle, lift first st of 3 sts just knit over last 2 sts; rep from * to last st, K1.

Row 2: With B, purl.

Stockinette Stitch

All RS rows: Knit.

All WS rows: Purl.

NOTE: When using hand-dyed yarn, remember to vary skeins throughout garment to maintain color quality.

Panels (make 2)

With longer needles and A, CO 66 sts. Work 18 (16, 18, 16) rows in St st.

With B, work 2 rows in eyelet patt.

With A, work 14 (16, 18, 20) rows in St st.

37, 40) sts. Working both sides at same time, BO 5 sts at each neck edge once. BO 4 sts at each neck edge once. BO 3 sts at each neck edge once. BO 2 sts at each neck edge once. Dec 1 st at each neck edge EOR 3 times—15 (17, 20, 23) sts. Work until piece measures 21 (22, 22, 23)". Place shoulder sts on holder.

Finishing

Knit shoulder seams tog, using 3-needle BO.

Armhole bands: With B, PU 90 (94, 98, 100) sts around armhole. Knit 3 rows. BO loosely in knit.

Sew side seams tog.

Neckband: With RS tog, using B and 16" circular needles, and beg at left shoulder seam, PU 21 (22, 22, 22) sts to front holder, K20 (22, 25, 26) sts from holder, PU 21 (22, 22, 22) sts

Rep, working 2 rows eyelet patt followed by 14 (16, 18, 20) rows St st, a total of 6 times.

Work 2 more rows in eyelet patt.

Work 18 (16, 18, 16) rows in St. st.

Yoke (make 1 front and 1 back)

With B, PU 108 (114, 123, 132) sts across selvage edge of panel. Purl next row. Work rows 1 and 2 of eyelet patt.

With A, work St st until piece measures 13 (13½, 13½, 14)".

Armhole shaping: Keeping continuity of patt, BO 4 sts at each side once. BO 3 sts at each side once. BO 2 sts at each side once. Dec 1 st at each side EOR 3 (3, 3, 4) times—84 (90, 99, 106) sts. Work until piece measures 18½ (19, 19, 20)".

Neck shaping: Keeping continuity of patt, work 32 (34, 37, 40) sts, place next 20 (22, 25, 26) sts on a holder. Join 2nd ball of yarn and work last 32 (34,

to shoulder seam, PU 21 (22, 22, 22) sts to back holder, K20 (22, 25, 26) sts from holder, PU 21 (22, 22, 22) sts to shoulder seam; PM and join. Work 3 rnds in garter st as foll:

Rnd 1: Purl.

Rnd 2: Knit.

Rnd 3: Purl.

BO loosely in knit.

Bottom band: With RS tog, using B and 24" circular needles, PU 192 (208, 224, 232) sts around bottom; PM and join. Work 3 rnds in garter st as foll:

Rnd 1: Purl.

Rnd 2: Knit.

Rnd 3: Purl.

BO loosely in knit.

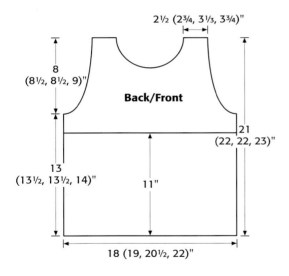

SLIP STITCH

SOMETIMES THE SIMPLEST THINGS can give tremendous rewards. The slip stitch is an incredibly simple stitch that changes the look and feel of a garment. The slip stitch has a multitude of benefits. When using hand-dyed yarn, the two most noticeable benefits are how this simple stitch impacts the texture and color placement in the garment.

The slip stitch alters the texture of the knitted fabric because stitches appear to be lifted from one row to other rows at varying lengths. Lifting the stitches in this manner breaks up straight lines of knitting and gives greater emphasis to the color of the slip stitches. Ultimately, the slip stitch lets you easily move color from one row to another, which is useful for breaking up the monotony of regular striping. With the slip stitch, straight lines appear blurred.

THERE ARE MANY DIFFERENT WAYS TO APPLY slip stitch. The two ways to make slip stitches will be discussed in this chapter—purlwise and knitwise. To do a purlwise slip stitch, insert the right-hand needle into the next stitch on the left-hand needle, as if to begin the next purl stitch, and slide the stitch onto the right-hand needle. Simply put, just move the yarn for the next stitch over without completing the stitch. Similarly, to do a knitwise slip stitch, insert the right-hand needle into the next stitch on the left-hand needle, as if to begin the next knit stitch, and slide the stitch onto the right-hand needle. Again, just move the yarn for the next stitch over without completing the stitch. Because you're inserting your needle from a different angle, the knitwise slip stitch actually twists the stitch so a different texture is created than with a purlwise slip stitch. Thus, you can easily use slip stitch, whether purling or knitting, to create different textures, depending on the main stitch you have chosen for your garment.

Using the slip stitch in conjunction with hand-dyed yarn enhances both the stitch and the yarn. If you like to work with monocolored yarn (hand-dyed yarn that is one color), use two different monocolors, and the slip stitch will break up the rigidity of the striping. Or try knitting with one monocolored yarn as the background and one multi-colored hand-dyed yarn. In this case, the slip stitch will highlight the variations in color provided by the multicolored yarn by lifting the color on top of the background color. You can also use the slip stitch when using two or three multicolored hand-dyed yarns. Here, the colors will be combined more completely, blurring the color changes as in an impressionist painting.

The four garments in this chapter illustrate how easily the slip stitch, when combined with two or more hand-dyed yarns, blends a variety of colors throughout the knitted fabric. Tundra Trail, Southern Cross, A Walk in the Garden, and Raging Reds all illustrate how hand-dyed yarn works effectively with the various ways to use slip stitch.

Tundra Trail

SKILL LEVEL: EASY ◼◼☐☐

TUNDRA TRAIL is a men's crewneck pullover. This heavy sweater was knit with one multicolored and four monocolored hand-dyed yarns. The monocolored yarns were knit in uniform stripes, while the multicolored yarn is knit throughout the garment, creating the appearance of ridges. The slip stitches are lifted over four rows, giving them a great deal of emphasis.

This richly colored men's sweater was knit using the hand-dyed yarns Kokopelli by Fiesta Yarns and Marjaana by Schaefer Yarn Company.

Finished Measurements

Chest: 40 (43½, 46½, 50, 53)"

Length: 24½ (25, 26, 26½, 27½)"

Materials

Fiesta DK Kokopelli (60% mohair, 40% wool; 165 yds/150 m, 4 oz per skein), in the following colors:

A 2 (2, 3, 4, 4) skeins of DK-22, Buckaroo Blue **4**

B 2 (2, 2, 3, 3) skeins of DK-13, Saddle Brown **4**

C 2 (2, 2, 3, 3) skeins of DK-12, Roasted Piñon **4**

D 2 (2, 2, 3, 3) skeins of DK-14, Squash Blossom **4**

Schaefer Marjaana (50% merino wool, 50% tussah silk; 550 yds/503 m, 8 oz per skein), in the following color:

E 2 (2, 3, 3, 3) skeins of Nancy Ward **4**

- Size US 6 (4 mm) needles or size required to obtain gauge
- Size US 6 (4 mm) 16" circular needles
- Size US 5 (3.75 mm) needles
- Stitch holders
- Stitch markers

Gauge

20 sts and 36 rows = 4" in patt on larger needles

To swatch, work 21 sts in patt but measure only 20 sts.

Ribbing Pattern

Row 1 (RS): *P1, K1; rep from * to last st, P1.

Row 2: *K1, P1; rep from * to last st, K1.

Stripe Pattern

Row 1 (RS): With B, K4, *K1 (wrapping yarn twice around needle), K3; rep from * to last st, K1.

Row 2: With B, P4, *sl 1 wyif (dropping wraps), P3; rep from * to last st, P1.

Row 3: With E, K4, *sl 1 wyib, K3; rep from * to last st, K1.

Row 4: With E, K4, *sl 1 wyif, K3; rep from * to last st, K1.

Row 5: With B, K2, *K1 (wrapping yarn twice around needle), K3; rep from * to last 3 sts, K1 (wrapping yarn twice around needle), K2.

NOTE: When using hand-dyed yarn, remember to vary skeins throughout garment to maintain color quality.

Back

With A and smaller needles, CO 93 (101, 109, 117, 125) sts. Work ribbing patt for 2¼", inc 8 sts evenly spaced across last WS row—101 (109, 117, 125, 133) sts.

Change to larger needles and work in stripe patt until piece measures 14½ (15, 15½, 16, 16½)".

Armhole shaping: Keeping continuity of patt, BO 2 sts at each side twice. Dec 1 st at each side EOR 4 (4, 4, 5, 5) times—85 (93, 101, 107, 115) sts. Work until piece measures 23½ (24, 25, 25½, 26½)".

Neck shaping: Keeping continuity of patt, work 29 (32, 34, 36, 38) sts, place next 27 (29, 33, 35, 39) sts on holder. Join 2nd ball of yarn and work last 29 (32, 34, 36, 38) sts. Working both sides at same time, BO 2 sts at each neck edge once—27 (30, 32, 34, 36) sts. Work until piece measures 24½ (25, 26,

Row 6: With B, P2, *sl 1 wyif (dropping wraps), P3; rep from * to last 3 sts, sl 1 wyif (dropping wraps), P2.

Row 7: With E, K2, *sl 1 wyib, K3; rep from * to last 3 sts, sl 1 wyib, K2.

Row 8: With E, K2, *sl 1 wyif, K3; rep from * to last 3 sts, sl 1 wyif, K2.

Rows 9–16: Rep rows 1–8.

Rows 17–32: Work rows 1–16 of patt, replacing color B with color C.

Rows 33–48: Work rows 1–16 of patt, replacing color B with color D.

Rows 49–64: Work rows 1–16 of patt, replacing color B with color A.

NOTE: Color E is worked in rows 3, 4, 7, and 8 throughout all 64 rows of patt.

26½, 27½)", ending on row 4, 8, 12, or 16 of patt. Knit 2 rows with E to stabilize the shoulder. Place shoulder sts on holder.

Front

Work as for back until piece measures 21½ (22, 22½, 23, 23½)".

Neck shaping: Keeping continuity of patt, work 36 (39, 42, 44, 46) sts, place next 13 (15, 17, 19, 23) sts on holder. Join 2nd ball of yarn and work last 36 (39, 42, 44, 46) sts. Working both sides at same time, BO 3 sts at each neck edge once. BO 2 sts at each neck edge twice. Dec 1 st at each neck edge EOR 2 (2, 3, 3, 3) times—27 (30, 32, 34, 36) sts. Work until piece measures 24½ (25, 26, 26½, 27)", ending on row 4, 8, 12, or 16 of patt. Knit 2 rows with E to stabilize shoulder. Place shoulder sts on holder.

Sleeves (make 2)

With A and smaller needles, CO 47 (47, 51, 51, 51) sts. Work ribbing patt for 2¼", inc 2 sts across last WS row—49 (49, 53, 53, 53) sts.

Change to larger needles and work in patt, inc 1 st at each side every 4th row 5 (5, 6, 6, 7) times—59 (59, 65, 65, 67) sts. Inc 1 st at each side every 6th row 20 times—99 (99, 105, 105, 107) sts. Work even until sleeve measures 17½ (18, 18½, 19, 19½)".

Cap shaping: Keeping continuity of patt, BO 2 sts at each side twice. Dec 1 st at each side EOR 4 (4, 4, 5, 5) times—83 (83, 89, 87, 89) sts. BO rem sts loosely.

Finishing

Knit shoulder seams tog, using 3-needle BO.

Sew in sleeves.

Sew side seams.

Neckband: With RS tog, A, and 16" circular needles, beg at left shoulder seam, PU 26 (26, 27, 27, 28) sts to front holder, K13 (15, 17, 19, 23) sts from holder, PU 26 (26, 27, 27, 28) sts to shoulder seam, PU 5 sts to back holder, K27 (29, 33, 35, 39) sts from holder, PU 5 sts to shoulder seam; PM and join. Work ribbing patt for 2¾". BO loosely in rib. Fold ribbing to inside and sew edge to inside neck edge.

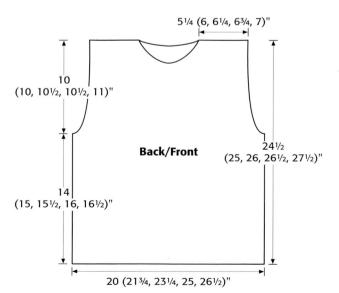

5¼ (6, 6¼, 6¾, 7)"

10 (10, 10½, 10½, 11)"

Back/Front

24½ (25, 26, 26½, 27½)"

14 (15, 15½, 16, 16½)"

20 (21¾, 23¼, 25, 26½)"

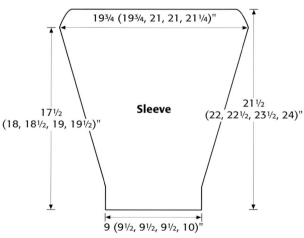

19¾ (19¾, 21, 21, 21¼)"

17½ (18, 18½, 19, 19½)"

Sleeve

21½ (22, 22½, 23½, 24)"

9 (9½, 9½, 9½, 10)"

Southern Cross

SKILL LEVEL: INTERMEDIATE ■■■□

 **SOUTHERN CROSS** is a women's V-neck vest. This everyday vest is perfect to wear with jeans and a T-shirt. Southern Cross is knit with two multicolored hand-dyed yarns using a slip-stitch cable pattern. The cabling moves the slip stitch to the right or the left, creating a diagonal effect rather than a vertical one. This multilayered vest is made with Southern Rose and Cross Connection by Wool in the Woods.

Finished Measurements

Bust: 38 (42, 46, 50, 54)"

Length: 21 (21½, 22, 23, 24)"

Materials

A 4 (4, 4, 5, 6) skeins of Wool in the Woods Southern Rose (55% mohair, 45% wool; 200 yds/183 m per skein), color Jam Jivin' **4**

B 2 (2, 3, 3, 4) skeins of Wool in the Woods Cross Connection (70% cotton, 30% nylon; 200 yds/183 m per skein), color Lottery **3**

• Size US 6 (4 mm) needles or size required to obtain gauge

• Size US 5 (3.75 mm) needles

• 7 (7, 7, 8, 8) buttons, ¾" diameter

• Cable needle

• Stitch holders

• Stitch markers

Gauge

24 sts and 30 rows = 4" in St st on larger needles

Ribbing Pattern

Row 1 (RS): *P2, K2; rep from * to last 2 sts, P2.

Row 2: *K2, P2; rep from * to last 2 sts, K2.

Slip-Stitch Cable Pattern

Row 1 (RS): With A, K2, *sl 2, K4; rep from * to last 4 sts, sl 2, K2.

Row 2: With A, P2, *sl 2, P4; rep from * to last 4 sts, sl 2, P2.

Row 3: With B, K1, C2F, C2B, *K2, C2F, C2B; rep from * to last st, K1.

Row 4: With B, purl.

Row 5: With A, K5, sl 2, *K4, sl 2; rep from * to last 5 sts, K5.

Row 6: With A, P5, *sl 2, P4; rep from * to last 7 sts, sl 2, P5.

Row 7: With B, K4, C2F, C2B, *K2, C2F, C2B; rep from * to last 4 sts, K4.

Row 8: With B, purl.

These 8 rows form patt.

Armhole shaping: Keeping continuity of patt, BO 4 sts at each armhole edge once. BO 3 sts at each armhole edge once. BO 2 sts at each armhole edge 1 (1, 1, 2, 2) times. Dec 1 st at each armhole edge EOR 3 times. Dec 1 st at each armhole edge every 4th row 3 times—84 (96, 108, 116, 128) sts. Work until piece measures 20 (20½, 21, 22, 23)".

Neck shaping: Keeping continuity of patt, work 25 (30, 35, 38, 43) sts, place next 34 (36, 38, 40, 42) sts on holder. Join 2nd ball of yarn and work last 25 (30, 35, 38, 43) sts. Working both sides at same time, BO 2 sts at each neck edge once. Work until piece measures 21 (21½, 22, 23, 24)". Place 23 (28, 33, 36, 41) shoulder sts on holder.

Fronts (work both pieces at same time)

With smaller needles and A, CO 58 (62, 70, 74, 82) sts for each front. Work ribbing as for back for 1¼". Change to larger needles and knit 1 row, inc 2 (4, 2, 4, 2) sts evenly across row—60 (66, 72, 78, 84) sts.

Abbreviations

C2B: Place next stitch on cable needle and hold at back of work. Knit next stitch and then knit stitch from cable needle.

C2F: Place next stitch on cable needle and hold at front of work. Knit next stitch and then knit stitch from cable needle.

NOTE: When using hand-dyed yarn, remember to vary skeins throughout garment to maintain color quality.

Back

With smaller needles and A, CO 110 (122, 134, 146, 158) sts. Work ribbing patt for 1¼". Change to larger needles. Knit next row, inc 4 sts evenly across row—114 (126, 138, 150, 162) sts.

Purl next row. Begin slip-stitch cable patt and work until piece measures 11½ (12, 12½, 13, 14)".

Purl next row. Begin slip-stitch cable patt and work in patt until pieces measure 11½ (12, 12½, 13, 14)".

Armhole and neck shaping: Keeping continuity of patt, work armhole shaping as for back. AT SAME TIME, dec 1 st at each neck edge EOR 0 (0, 3, 6, 9) times. Dec 1 st at each neck edge every 4th row to 23 (28, 33, 36, 41) sts. Work until pieces measure 21 (21½, 22, 23, 24)".

Finishing

Knit shoulder seams tog, using 3-needle BO.

Armhole bands: With RS tog, A, and smaller needles, PU 150 (158, 158, 162, 162) sts. Work ribbing as for back for 8 rows. BO in ribbing patt.

Sew side seams tog.

Front and neckbands: On right front, place 7 (7, 7, 8, 8) markers evenly spaced from V-neck to bottom for buttonholes. With RS tog, A, and smaller needles, PU 77 (82, 83, 86, 89) sts from bottom right front to V-neck, PU 80 (80, 80, 82, 82) sts to shoulder seam, PU 5 sts to back holder, K34 (36, 38, 40, 42) sts from back holder, PU 5 sts to shoulder seam, PU 80 (80, 80, 82, 82) sts to front V-neck, PU 77 (82, 83, 86, 89) sts to bottom left front. Work ribbing as for back for 3 rows. Work 7 (7, 7, 8, 8) buttonholes evenly spaced at markers over next 2 rows of rib (see "Buttonholes" on page 17). Work 2 more rows in rib. BO in knit.

Sew buttons to left front band.

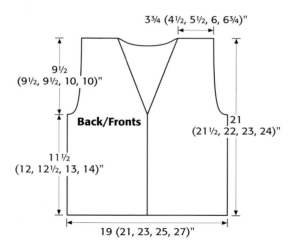

3¾ (4½, 5½, 6, 6¾)"

9½ (9½, 9½, 10, 10)"

Back/Fronts

21 (21½, 22, 23, 24)"

11½ (12, 12½, 13, 14)"

19 (21, 23, 25, 27)"

A Walk in the Garden

A WALK IN THE GARDEN is a women's crewneck sweater. What could be lovelier than picking fall flowers in a sweater that is as enticing as the colors in your own garden? A Walk in the Garden was knit with a slip-stitch pattern using three multicolored yarns, two of which are stranded together. The slip stitch occurs on the right side of the knitted fabric. The pattern for this sweater requires that you change yarn every two rows.

This well-blended sweater is made of the yarns Possum Paints Worsted by Cherry Tree Hill Yarn plus Feel'n Fuzzy and Cherub by Wool in the Woods.

Finished Measurements

Bust: 37½ (40½, 44, 47, 50)"

Length: 21 (21½, 22 ½, 23½, 24½)"

Materials

A 7 (7, 8, 9, 10) skeins of Cherry Tree Hill Possum Paints Worsted (70% superwash merino, 30% possum; 109 yds/100 m, 50 g per skein), color Indian Summer **(4)**

B 3 (3, 4, 4, 5) skeins of Wool in the Woods Feel'n Fuzzy (90% mohair, 10% nylon; 200 yds/183 m per skein), color Grandma's Garden **(1)**

C 3 (3, 4, 4, 5) skeins of Wool in the Woods Cherub (100% wool; 200 yds/183 m per skein), color Uptown **(1)**

• Size US 6 (4 mm) needles or size required to obtain gauge

• Size US 5 (3.75 mm) needles

• Size US 5 (3.75 mm) 16" circular needles

• Stitch holders

• Stitch markers

Gauge

20 sts and 28 rows = 4" in patt on larger needles

To swatch, work 22 sts in patt but measure only 20 sts.

Ribbing Pattern

Row 1 (RS): *P1, K1; rep from * to last st, P1.

Row 2: *K1, P1; rep from * to last st, K1.

Slip-Stitch Pattern

Row 1 (RS): With B and C held tog, K1, *K3, sl 1 wyif; rep from * to last st, K1.

Row 2: With B and C held tog, purl.

Row 3: With A, K1, *K2, sl 1 wyif, K1; rep from * to last st, K1.

Row 4: With A, purl.

Row 5: With B and C held tog, K1, *K1, sl 1 wyif, K2; rep from * to last st, K1.

Row 6: With B and C held tog, purl.

Row 7: With A, K1, *sl 1 wyif, K3; rep from * to last st, K1.

Row 8: With A, purl.

These 8 rows form patt.

NOTE: When using hand-dyed yarn, remember to vary skeins throughout garment to maintain color quality.

Back

With A and smaller needles, CO 87 (95, 103, 111, 119) sts. Work ribbing patt for 1½", inc 7 sts evenly spaced across last WS row—94 (102, 110, 118, 126) sts.

Change to larger needles and work in slip-st patt until piece measures 12 (12, 13, 13½, 14½)".

Armhole shaping: Keeping continuity of patt, BO 2 sts at each side once. Dec 1 st at each side EOR 3 (3, 3, 4, 4) times—84 (92, 100, 106, 114) sts. Work until piece measures 20 (20½, 21½, 22½, 23½)".

Neck shaping: Keeping continuity of patt, work 28 (31, 34, 36, 39) sts, place next 28 (30, 32, 34, 36)

sts on holder. Join 2nd ball of yarn and work last 28 (31, 34, 36, 39) sts. Working both sides at same time, BO 2 sts at each neck edge once—26 (29, 32, 34, 37) sts. Work until piece measures 21 (21½, 22½, 23½, 24½)". Place shoulder sts on holder.

Front

Work as for back until piece measures 18 (18, 19, 20, 20½)".

Neck shaping: Keeping continuity of patt, work 35 (38, 41, 43, 46) sts, place next 14 (16, 18, 20, 22) sts on holder. Join 2nd ball of yarn and work last 35 (38, 41, 43, 46) sts. Working both sides at same time, BO 3 sts at each neck edge once. BO 2 sts at each neck edge once. Dec 1 st at each neck edge EOR 4 times—26 (29, 32, 34, 37) sts. Work until piece measures 21 (21½, 22½, 23½, 24½)". Place shoulder sts on holder.

Sleeves (make 2)

With A and smaller needles, CO 41 (41, 41, 45, 45) sts. Work ribbing for 1½", inc 1 st on last WS row—42 (42, 42, 46, 46) sts.

Change to larger needles and work in slip-st patt, inc 1 st at each side every 6th row 4 times—50 (50, 50, 54, 54) sts. Inc 1 st at each side every 4th row 15 (16, 16, 17, 17) times—80 (82, 82, 88, 88) sts. Work even until sleeve measures 16 (16, 17, 17, 18)".

Cap shaping: Keeping continuity of patt, BO 2 sts at each side once. Dec 1 st at each side EOR 3 (3, 3, 4, 4) times—70 (72, 72, 76, 76) sts. BO remaining sts loosely.

Finishing

Knit shoulder seams tog, using 3-needle BO.

Sew in sleeves.

Sew side seams.

Neckband: With RS tog, A, and 16" circular needles, beg at left shoulder seam, PU 27 sts to front holder, K14 (16, 18, 20, 22) sts from holder, PU 27 sts to shoulder seam, PU 7 sts to back holder, K28 (30, 32, 34, 36) sts from holder, PU 7 sts to shoulder seam; PM and join. Work ribbing patt for 1½". BO loosely in ribbing.

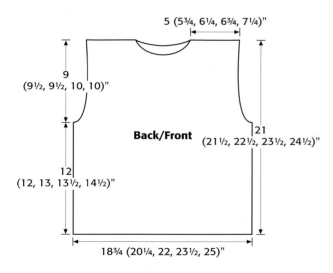

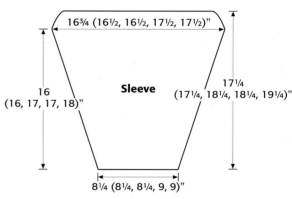

Raging Reds

SKILL LEVEL: INTERMEDIATE ■■■□

 RAGING REDS is a women's belted ruana with I-cord edging. We used one multicolored hand-dyed yarn along with a solid-colored yarn (not hand dyed) to show you how effectively you can use solid yarn in a garment as a background for the more glamorous hand-dyed yarn. To create depth, we used the linen stitch for the ruana, and as usual, changed skeins of the hand-dyed yarn every two rows.

This radiant garment was knit with 14-ply wool yarn by Baabajoes Wool Company.

Finished Measurements

Bust: 34 (36, 38, 40)"

Length: 24 (24, 24½, 25)"

NOTE: Choose a size approximately 4" smaller than your normal finished measurement; otherwise, the ruana will be too large at the shoulders, creating unwanted "wings."

Materials

Baabajoes Wool Company, 14-ply (100% wool; 310 yds/284 m, 250 g per skein), in the following colors:

A 1 (2, 2, 2) skein(s) of Black **5**

B 1 (1, 2, 2) skein(s) of Fire **5**

- Size US 10½ (6.5 mm) needles or size required to obtain gauge

- Size US 10 (6 mm) double-pointed needles

- Stitch holder

Gauge

16 sts and 24 rows = 4" in patt on larger needles

Linen Stitch

Row 1 (RS): With A, *K1, sl 1 pw wyif; rep from * to end.

Row 2: With A, *P1, sl 1 pw wyib; rep from * to end.

Row 3: With B, work row 1.

Row 4: With A, work row 2.

These 4 rows form patt.

NOTE: When using hand-dyed yarn, remember to vary skeins throughout garment to maintain color quality.

Back

With A and larger needles, CO 68 (72, 76, 80) sts. Work patt until piece measures 24 (24, 24½, 25)". Place sts on holder.

Fronts (work both pieces at same time)

With A and larger needles, CO 34 (36, 38, 40) sts for each front. Work in patt as for back until pieces measure 10 (10, 10½, 11)".

Neck shaping: Keeping continuity of patt, dec 1 st at each neck edge every 6th row 12 times—22 (24, 26, 28) sts. Work in patt until pieces measure 24 (24, 24½, 25)".

Finishing

Knit shoulder seams tog, using 3-needle BO and binding off center 24 sts.

Using dpn, work attached I-cord edging around fronts and sides as foll: Using A and smaller double-pointed needles, PU 1 st in bottom right front. CO 3 sts using the picked-up st. K2, K2tog tbl. PU 1 st on right front. Slide needle to other end, K2, K2tog tbl. Cont in this manner to end.

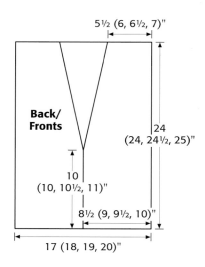

5½ (6, 6½, 7)"

Back/ Fronts

24 (24, 24½, 25)"

10 (10, 10½, 11)"

8½ (9, 9½, 10)"

17 (18, 19, 20)"

Abbreviations

beg	beginning		oz	ounce(s)
BO	bind off		P	purl
CO	cast on		pw	purlwise
C2B	place next stitch on cable needle and hold at back of work; knit next stitch and then knit stitch from cable needle		patt	pattern
			PM	place marker
			PU	pick up and knit
C2F	place next stitch on cable needle and hold at front of work; knit next stitch and then knit stitch from cable needle		P2tog	purl 2 stitches together
			P3tog	purl 3 stitches together
			rem	remain/remaining
cont	continue		rep	repeat
dec	decrease/decreases/decreasing		rev St st	reverse stockinette stitch
dpn	double-pointed needles		rnd(s)	round(s)
EOR	every other row		RS	right side(s)
est	established		sc	single crochet
foll	follow/follows/following		sl	slip
g	gram		st(s)	stitch(es)
garter st	garter stitch		ssk	slip 1, slip 1, knit these 2 stitches together—a decrease
inc	increase/increases/increasing		ssp	slip 1, slip 1, purl these 2 stitches together—a decrease
K1tbl	knit 1 stitch through back loop			
K1 in st below	insert the needle into the center of the stitch below the next stitch on the needle and knit in the usual way, slipping the stitch above it off the needle at the same time		St st	stockinette stitch/stocking stitch
			tbl	through the back loop
			tog	together
K	knit		WS	wrong side
K2tog	knit 2 stitches together		wyib	with yarn in back
K3tog	knit 3 stitches together		wyif	with yarn in front
kw	knitwise		yo	yarn over
m	meter(s)			
mm	millimeter			

Useful Information

Measurement Conversions

To easily convert yards to meters or vice versa for calculating how much yarn you'll need for your project, use these handy formulas.

ounces = grams × 0.0352

grams = ounces × 28.35

yards = meters × 1.0936

meters = yards × 0.914

Standard Yarn-Weight System

Yarn-Weight Symbol and Category Names	1 SUPER FINE	2 FINE	3 LIGHT	4 MEDIUM	5 BULKY	6 SUPER BULKY
Type of Yarns in Category	Sock, fingering, baby	Sport, baby	DK, light worsted	Worsted, afghan, Aran	Chunky, craft, rug	Bulky, roving
Knit Gauge Range in St st to 4"	27 to 32	23 to 26	21 to 24	16 to 20	12 to 15	6 to 11

Skill Levels

■□□□ **Beginner:** Projects for first-time knitters using basic knit and purl stitches. Minimal shaping.

■■□□ **Easy:** Projects using basic stitches, repetitive stitch patterns, and simple color changes. Simple shaping and finishing.

■■■□ **Intermediate:** Projects using a variety of stitches, such as basic cables and lace, simple intarsia, and techniques for double-pointed needles and knitting in the round. Mid-level shaping and finishing.

■■■■ **Experienced:** Projects using advanced techniques and stitches, such as short rows, Fair Isle, more intricate intarsia, cables, lace patterns, and numerous color changes.

Resources

Baabajoes Wool Company
PO Box 260604
Lakewood, CO 80226
(303) 239-6313
www.baabajoeswool.com

Blue Heron Yarns
29532 Canvasback Dr. #6
Easton, MD 21601
(410) 819-0401
www.blueheronyarns.com

Blue Sky Alpacas, Inc.
PO Box 387
St. Francis, MN 55070
www.blueskyalpacas.com

Cherry Tree Hill Yarn
PO Box 659
Barton, VT 05022
(802) 525-3311
www.cherryyarn.com

Dancing Fibers
509 N. Hillford Ave.
Compton, CA 90220
(510) 530-8174
www.dancingfibers.com

EK Success, Ltd.
125 Entin Rd.
Clifton, NJ 07014
(800) 524-1349
www.eksuccess.com

Fiesta Yarns
206 Frontage Rd.
Rio Rancho, NM 87124
(505) 892-5008
www.fiestayarns.com

The Great Adirondack Yarn Company
950 Co. Hwy. 126
Amsterdam, NY 10210
(518) 843-3381

Lorna's Laces
4229 N. Honore St.
Chicago, IL 60613
(773) 935-3803
www.lornaslaces.net

Mountain Colors
PO Box 156
Corvallis, MT 59828
(406) 777-3377
www.mountaincolors.com

Prism Arts, Inc.
3140 39th Ave. N.
St. Petersburg, FL 33714
(727) 327-3100

Schaefer Yarn Company
3514 Kelly's Corner Rd.
Interlaken, NY 14847
(607) 532-9452
www.schaeferyarn.com

Skacel Collection, Inc.
PO Box 88110
Seattle, WA 98138-2110
(253) 854-2710
www.skacelknitting.com

Wool in the Woods
58 Scarlet Way
Biglerville, PA 17307
(717) 677-0577
www.woolinthewoods.com

New and Bestselling Titles from

Martingale®
& C O M P A N Y

America's Best-Loved Craft & Hobby Books®
America's Best-Loved Knitting Books®

That Patchwork Place®

America's Best-Loved Quilt Books®

NEW RELEASES
300 Paper-Pieced Quilt Blocks
American Doll Quilts
Classic Crocheted Vests
Dazzling Knits
Follow-the-Line Quilting Designs
Growing Up with Quilts
Hooked on Triangles
Knitting with Hand-Dyed Yarns
Lavish Lace
Layer by Layer
Lickety-Split Quilts
Magic of Quiltmaking, The
More Nickel Quilts
More Reversible Quilts
No-Sweat Flannel Quilts
One-of-a-Kind Quilt Labels
Patchwork Showcase
Pieced to Fit
Pillow Party!
Pursenalities
Quilter's Bounty
Quilting with My Sister
Seasonal Quilts Using Quick Bias
Two-Block Appliqué Quilts
Ultimate Knitted Tee, The
Vintage Workshop, The
WOW! Wool-on-Wool Folk-Art Quilts

KNITTING
Basically Brilliant Knits
Beyond Wool
Classic Knitted Vests
Comforts of Home
Dazzling Knits **NEW!**
Fair Isle Sweaters Simplified
Garden Stroll, A
Knit it Now!
Knits for Children and Their Teddies
Knits from the Heart
Knitted Shawls, Stoles, and Scarves
Knitted Throws and More
Knitter's Book of Finishing Techniques, The
Knitter's Template, A
Knitting with Hand-Dyed Yarns **NEW!**
Knitting with Novelty Yarns
Lavish Lace **NEW!**
Little Box of Scarves, The
Little Box of Sweaters, The
More Paintbox Knits

Pursenalities **NEW!**
Simply Beautiful Sweaters
Simply Beautiful Sweaters for Men
Style at Large
Too Cute!
Treasury of Rowan Knits, A
Ultimate Knitted Tee, The **NEW!**
Ultimate Knitter's Guide, The

CROCHET
Classic Crocheted Vests **NEW!**
Crochet for Babies and Toddlers
Crochet for Tots
Crocheted Aran Sweaters
Crocheted Lace
Crocheted Socks!
Crocheted Sweaters
Today's Crochet

CRAFTS
20 Decorated Baskets
Beaded Elegance
Blissful Bath, The
Collage Cards
Creating with Paint
Holidays at Home
Pretty and Posh
Purely Primitive
Stamp in Color
Trashformations
Warm Up to Wool
Year of Cats…in Hats!, A

APPLIQUÉ
Appliquilt in the Cabin
Blossoms in Winter
Garden Party
Shadow Appliqué
Stitch and Split Appliqué
Sunbonnet Sue All through the Year

LEARNING TO QUILT
101 Fabulous Rotary-Cut Quilts
Happy Endings, Revised Edition
Loving Stitches, Revised Edition
More Fat Quarter Quilts
Quilter's Quick Reference Guide, The
Sensational Settings, Revised Edition
Simple Joys of Quilting, The
Your First Quilt Book (or it should be!)

PAPER PIECING
40 Bright and Bold Paper-Pieced Blocks
50 Fabulous Paper-Pieced Stars
Down in the Valley
Easy Machine Paper Piecing
For the Birds
Papers for Foundation Piecing
Quilter's Ark, A
Show Me How to Paper Piece
Traditional Quilts to Paper Piece

QUILTS FOR BABIES & CHILDREN
Easy Paper-Pieced Baby Quilts
Easy Paper-Pieced Miniatures
Even More Quilts for Baby
More Quilts for Baby
Quilts for Baby
Sweet and Simple Baby Quilts

ROTARY CUTTING/SPEED PIECING
365 Quilt Blocks a Year Perpetual Calendar
1000 Great Quilt Blocks
Burgoyne Surrounded
Clever Quarters
Clever Quilts Encore
Endless Stars
Once More around the Block
Pairing Up
Stack a New Deck
Star-Studded Quilts
Strips and Strings
Triangle-Free Quilts

Our books are available at bookstores and your favorite craft, fabric, and yarn retailers. If you don't see the title you're looking for, visit us at
www.martingale-pub.com
or contact us at:
1-800-426-3126
International: 1-425-483-3313
Fax: 1-425-486-7596
Email: info@martingale-pub.com